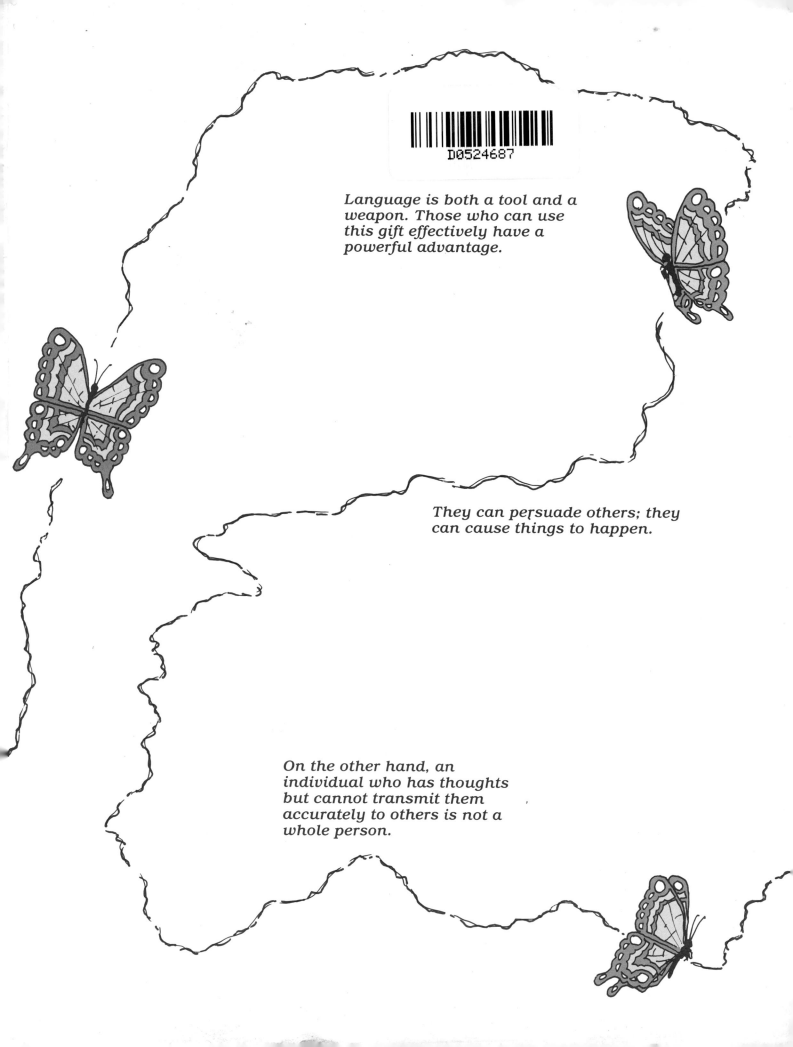

Language is both a tool and a weapon. Those who can use this gift effectively have a powerful advantage.

They can persuade others; they can cause things to happen.

On the other hand, an individual who has thoughts but cannot transmit them accurately to others is not a whole person.

About the Author

President of International Writing Institute, Mr. Joseph has almost certainly taught more people how to write than any other educator or writer who ever lived. He is the author of *Put It In Writing*, by far the most widely used writing course in the English-speaking world. He has been described as "... the most vocal of a small band of pioneering educators crusading for clear, readable English." His concepts go beyond business writing; he believes that anything written—whether a government regulation or a great novel—should be understandable. He has no patience with "windbags," as he calls unclear writers, in the world of work, academia, or literature.

For a large part of his life, Mr. Joseph was editor-in-chief of a national business magazine. He has also been a member of the faculty of Case Western Reserve University and guest lecturer at several other universities, and is an authority on the special problems of government writing.

He received national acclaim for his uniquely successful approach to teaching writing when his course was produced as a videotaped series by the National Educational Television Network. He is also author of *The New English*, an experimental course in English composition for children. He is former chairman of the board of directors of Plain Talk, Inc., a public interest group promoting the use of plain English in business and government documents.

Executive Guide to Grammar was written as a result of popular demand after years of request from admirers of *Put It in Writing*.

Executive Guide to Grammar

by Albert Joseph

© International Writing Institute, Inc., 1984, 1985, 1987
Library of Congress Catalog Card Number 82-084293
ISBN 0-911481-00-1

juui

Published by: International Writing Institute, Inc.–Cleveland, Ohio
Printed in the United States of America

Third Edition

Foreword

Why so small a book on so large a subject?

As an educator, I believe firmly that any educator's job is to make learning as easy as possible. As a writer and admirer of good writing, I believe the expository writer's job is to tell as much as possible, as clearly and accurately as possible, in as little reading as possible. I believe there is something terribly wrong with the "*here-it-is-if-you're-good-enough*" attitude displayed by so many educators and writers.

If you have ever taken or considered taking an adult education course, or attended a seminar or workshop, you have probably said: "It will be worth the time and effort if I get a few important ideas." You should get more than that out of this study program.

This is *not* a definitive treatise on grammar. You can find scores of those, many excellent, in any library or bookstore. Their trouble is they cover too much; the few most important ideas are made inaccessible—buried among pages and pages of details. Important and unimportant are treated alike, and the poor reader must decide for himself or herself what is important and what is merely nice to know.

In this book those things have been decided for you, and that is why the book is so short. You should learn more, not less, as a result.

A. J.
Cleveland, Ohio
1987

TO DYLENE, who made this book happen.

SPECIAL THANKS to the men and women of the United States Navy Fleet and Mine Warfare Training Center, Charleston, South Carolina, who tested this book in classrooms before it was published and helped in its instructional design.

Preface

THE FIRST WRITING was business writing. Tablets found in archeological digs of ancient Sumeria and Egypt, carved some 5,000 years ago, were records of the transfer of goods and property. Writing of religious and civil laws came slightly later, followed by writing to inform or to entertain.

Spoken language is much older—probably as old as human society. Many linguists and anthropologists believe, in fact, that human society began as our prehistoric ancestors developed the ability to transmit their thoughts by making sounds. Grunts became words, then sentences, and a new animal rose above the others and dominated the surface of the earth.

What is Grammar?

It is a set of rules, really, for using a language. Its purpose is to help people understand each other by requiring them to follow the *same* rules—to use the language as closely as possible to the same way. You might compare grammar to traffic signals. Everywhere in the world, a green light means *go* and red means *stop*. Such rules exist only because PEOPLE decided they would be useful and created them, and they are useful only to the extent people agree to follow them.

Almost all of these rules are based on *the sentence*. (Indeed, in language as in traffic, the most important signs are *go* [capital letter] and *stop* [period]). Few things in grammar go beyond a sentence; almost everything serves to regulate the arrangement of words and punctuation marks between one capital letter and its accompanying period. The noble purpose of it all: to broadcast the idea you are trying to convey in that sentence so clearly your reader (or listener) receives exactly and only that idea. If you can do that, you can write any idea your brain is capable of creating—whether it's a business report or the great American novel.

How Do We Learn It?

At first, by picking up language patterns from our home environment. You probably learned some formal rules in school, but much of our knowledge of grammar comes to us intuitively, beginning in infancy. By the time the young child begins to talk, his or her brain has already recognized basic language patterns and learned to mimic them. (For example: Even before they have learned to talk, babies in English-speaking cultures have learned to recognize the differences between *I, me*, and *my*. The youngest child says "*I* want . . . " but "Give *me* . . . " and "*My* doggie . . . ")

Whatever language patterns the child is exposed to in that home environment, he or she will learn as "correct"—whether the Old English of *Beowulf*, the aristocratic English of Oxford, the nonstandard English or street talk of some American minority groups, or one of the many dialects of Sinhalese spoken in Sri Lanka.

What Makes Grammar Correct?

Perhaps "correct" is the wrong word; most language scholars agree that "acceptance" of a language style is more relevant than whether one style or usage is "better" than another.

Whether you prefer "He be's the coolest" or "Ontogeny recapitulates phylogeny," you really don't accomplish much by arguing which is better language usage. Each may be better *in its own environment*, and social or professional groups develop their own language styles and guard them jealously.

More important than "Which is better," then, is the question: "Which language style will get you what you want?"

Who Decides What's "Standard"?

The public, really. That is, the people with clout. But they are not the authors, the television writers, the speech makers, or the many others who create the things we read and hear. Rather, the people who read and listen to them are the ones who have the real clout—who determine what is or is not acceptable. Whether for a scholarly dissertation or a beer commercial, the author's choice of language style is influenced by those who must respond to it.

Linguists and scholars do identify a style they call "standard English." It is a moderate style, somewhat between academia and beer-macho, and it is the style used by most newspapers, magazines, and radio or television stations. (There is a reason for this: It appeals to the largest number of people.) It derives its solid foundation from the rules of English grammar and usage as they have been collected and examined by such experts as H.W. Fowler, Otto Jespersen, and most recently such writers as William Safire, John Simon, and William and Mary Morris.

Why Does It Matter Whether You Follow Rules, If People Understand You?

It matters for two reasons. First, the way you use language tells people much more than just the message you are trying to convey. Like your clothes, or the way you wear your hair, your language style makes a strong unspoken statement about you. If your words and sentences do not quite follow the group's rules, people in that group will question your intelligence—or your ability to do your job. They *shouldn't*, you may argue; and you are probably right. But they *will*—whether they should or not. Likewise, if your language does follow the group's standards, members of the group are likely to take a more kindly attitude and presume (at first, anyhow) that you are intelligent and capable—whether you are or not. They will welcome your ideas with greater respect than if your language style is not what they consider to be the "in" style. In the business and academic worlds, then, those whose language style follows the rules of standard English grammar always have a major advantage. *Remember: Whether it is fair or not, in any group you are judged as much on HOW you say things as on WHAT you say.*

Second, careful language is usually a sign of careful thinking. Obviously, you must *think* an idea clearly before you can *express* it clearly. Less obvious, however, is the opposite: Expressing the idea also helps you to think it out clearly. Here's why: The brain monitors its ideas best when it can *see* them—literally, through its eyes. Reading its own output helps your brain to spot weaknesses in its thinking that it would not otherwise notice, and to correct them.

Language skill, then, will first of all give others the impression you are a person of merit. It will also help you think clearly and, therefore, to present your ideas in a clear, well-organized, hard-hitting way. Whether people say, "The dude is cool" or "This is a person whose ideas we should value," they are likely to be right.

Table of Contents

"Sloppy writing instantly
reveals the sloppy mind."

—*James J. Kilpatrick*

About English

About English

the 4,000 known languages, English is the native tongue of more people (approximately 600 million) than any other except Mandarin Chinese. In the number who employ it as their native *or second* language, it is by far the most widely used—and rapidly increasing its lead. It is truly the international language of politics (replacing French), science (replacing German), education (replacing Latin), commerce, and the arts.

Its emergence as the world's dominant language is due in part, of course, to recent world history; British and American political interests, and American business ingenuity, have carried English to every remote part of the world. And wherever it has gone, our language has carried with it the concept of freedom. But a large part of the credit must go to the language itself. English is a remarkable language with a fascinating history and an unlikely combination of diverse characteristics. Its vocabulary and structure offer a wide choice of images and rhythms to satisfy the poets; its efficiency provides scientists and engineers the precise expression they need; and, at the same time, its simple grammar and words (yes, they are) make it easy to learn—and the ideal language for plain talk in complex documents.

Its History

English is in the broad category of languages known as Indo-European. Its origin goes back about 2,500 years. Probably the one influence that most contributed to its development was military occupation. Historians divide its development into four important periods: Pre-English (roughly 500 B.C. to 500 A.D.), Old English (500 to 1100 A.D.), Middle English (1100 to 1500), and Modern English (1500 to present). Dictionaries refer to these as PreE, OE, ME, and ModE.

Its Celtic Roots—The first inhabitants of Britain that historians know much about were the Celts, who migrated approximately 500 B.C. from the part of continental Europe called Gaul (later to become France). Historians generally refer to the people as Celtic and their language as Gaelic. This language does not at all resemble English or French, but it was the beginning of both. (It is still recognizable in the dialects of Scotland, Ireland, and Wales—and the French province of Brittany.)

The Romans invaded Britain in 43 A.D. and occupied it and influenced every facet of its culture for several centuries. Under Roman rule, the Celts (who now called themselves Britons) probably enjoyed greater security, freedom, and comfort than English peoples in any period until very recent history. But Roman soldiers apparently did not socialize much with the Britons; we assume this because the Gaelic language in Britain did not pick up many traces of Latin. (In Gaul it did; that is why French is one of the Romance languages and English is not.) Roman rulers did, however, impose their alphabet on the Britons. It was an unfortunate legacy, as the 26-letter Roman alphabet does not fit the 43 sounds of English very well.

The Celts produced no significant writers or poets. Greek and Roman authors of this period were creating works of such wisdom and beauty that they still endure as classical literature and probably will forever. But we know of no important Celtic writing or writers.

Old English (500 to 1100 A.D.)—"The cantons should take steps to defend themselves." With these words in the year 410, the Emperor Honorius issued warning of the decline and fall of the Roman Empire. Most of Europe would enter a six-hundred-year period known as the Dark Ages. And the Anglo-Saxon (OE) period of British history was about to begin.

As Rome's economy weakened and its armies throughout Europe could no longer control the occupied lands, European tribes again dared to cross the English Channel, following the trek the Celts and Romans had taken centuries earlier, and Britain was invaded again. This time the invaders were Vikings. They came up the rivers in their long boats first just to plunder and to take home gold and jewels from the churches. But gradually they learned that this warm, gentle island provided an easier life than their native lands of northern Europe, and they came to stay. The most durable of these were the Angles (who gave England its name), Saxons, Picts, Frisians, and Jutes. They were Teutonic peoples, from the area that is now northern Germany, Holland, and Denmark. Their languages were Germanic and would blend with the Gaelic of the native Britons, to form the beginning of English. *Old English, then, is a mixture of Gaelic and Teutonic.*

But the Viking marauders, after they became settlers, were interested mostly in farming; therefore, they did not pursue the native Britons who pulled back into the mountainous, less hospitable areas to the west (Wales) or north (Scotland), or across the straits to Ireland. In those areas, as a result, the two cultures and languages did not mix. That is why, today, Gaelic is still very evident in the Welsh, Scotch, and Irish dialects.

The Anglo-Saxon period is the period of King Arthur and the Knights of the Round Table. (Most historians believe they existed and fought fiercely against early Viking plunderers.) More notable kings were Alfred the Great, Aethelred the Unready, Canute (or Cnut), and Harthcanute. But the most famous of all was the last of the Anglo-Saxon kings, Edward the Confessor, who set the stage for the events that unfolded one October day of 1066 outside a village called Hastings.

The outstanding literary work of the Old English period is the epic poem *Beowulf*, an adventure story of heroes and dragons, written about 700 A.D. by Anglo-Saxon monks. It is not a particularly engaging story, but it is important because it tells us a great deal about life and beliefs in those times. The language is so different from Modern English, however, that an untrained reader could not possibly understand *Beowulf* without help from a specialist.

Middle English (1100 to 1500)—The Norman period. British Kings in the Old English (Anglo-Saxon) period reigned over a shaky empire. Powerful dukes and earls ruled large areas, commanding their own armies of feudal serfs, and they could usually influence the kings or ignore them. By the time of Edward the Confessor, however, the power structure was changing and England had become, to a large extent, a unified nation. Edward was a beloved king, deeply religious. (He built Westminster Abbey and several other cathedrals.) But he and Queen Edith had no children. There was widespread fear that civil war would erupt among the noblemen to determine who would be king if he died without a successor, and so he was pressured to name one. Edward had strong ties to Normandy, a northern neighbor of France and today part of France. He had been raised there (in exile), and his mother was a Norman. In 1051 he named his cousin William, Duke of Normandy, to succeed him on his death as King of England. But before dying in January, 1066, Edward named another cousin, Harold Godwin, to be king. Harold II, not Edward the Confessor, was actually the last of the Anglo-Saxon kings—but for such a short time that few people know of him. He was Edward's brother-in-law, son of the powerful Earl of Wessex (the Kingmaker), and it is likely that Wessex ruled for the dying king and made the appointment himself.

One of the best-known passages in all of literature is Shakespeare's "Oh Romeo, Romeo! wherefore art thou Romeo?" Yet, most people misinterpret it.

Juliet is not asking "Where are you, Romeo?" She's asking "*Why* are you Romeo?" (Why couldn't you have been someone else, so our families wouldn't be feuding? —a bit of self-pity.)

That passage is a good example of the changes that constantly

Poor Harold II (there has never been a Harold III). Evidence suggests he might have been an able king, but he did not live long enough to prove it. Two things prevented it: (1) the Vikings were restless again, and (2) the Duke of Normandy was, to say the least, unhappy at the appointment.

Vikings who had stayed in Scandinavia (and now called themselves Danes) had never completely stopped their raids on the earlier Vikings who had migrated across the Channel (and now called themselves Englishmen). In fact, Anglo-Saxon kings often paid heavy ransoms of gold (called Danegeld) to buy peace. Edward's death was an invitation for the Danes to step up their harrassment, to test the new king. They invaded from the north in the summer of 1066, and Harold considered them a serious threat.

But the second threat would prove more serious, and it too was of Viking origin.

During the social, political, and military turmoil of the Dark Ages, in the power vacuum created when Rome lost control, restless Vikings migrated on the European continent as well as across the English Channel. Some marauded and settled down the coast as far as the northern part of Gaul (France). Here they were called Northmen, or "Norman," and the land they settled became Normandy.[1]

The Duke of Normandy, then, had ancient Viking ties. One way or the other, Harold could not escape his Viking end.

When Edward the Confessor died, his cousin William, Duke of Normandy, considered himself the rightful King of England. Edward had, after all, proclaimed him successor; William refused to acknowledge the later appointment of Harold Godwin and considered him a pretender. Furthermore, William was a blood relative while Harold was related by marriage. In the autumn of 1066, the Norman armies crossed the English Channel from Calais and landed at Dover, three miles from their rendezvous with destiny.

Harold had just staged a major victory over the Danes; now he turned his armies southward, confident they would repel the Normans. The two forces met on Friday, October 13, at Hastings. Their outcome still affects the shape of nations and cultures today.

Did Harold push his inexperienced armies too fast, and were they therefore unprepared for the disciplined and well-rested Normans? Maybe. Was the arrow that smashed Harold's brain through his right eye a lucky shot? Almost certainly. Military scholars believe, however, that the outcome of the Battle of Hastings had been determined before the armies met—by a technological breakthrough as significant then as nuclear weapons are today: *the stirrup*.

Both sides knew of these new leather straps with footloops, but the Normans were first to equip an army with them. Norman horsemen, then, had a major and unexpected advantage: they could hold their grip on the horse with their legs, freeing both hands in combat; this allowed them to wield a sword or ax *and at the same time protect themselves with a shield*. The battle lasted one day, and on that day William, Duke of Normandy, became known forever as William the Conqueror.

The Norman Conquest, however, was much more than just the Battle of Hastings. Large parts of England were under the rule of feudal lords who traditionally had little loyalty to the king, and the Conqueror was determined to bring *all* of England under his absolute rule. In the ensuing years, Norman knights rode through the land on a relentless campaign to eliminate every possible source of opposition. All noble or otherwise prominent or influential families were executed. Burning of villages, painful

---

1. In Gaul, as in Britain, Gaelic and Teutonic dialects met and combined to form a new language. Why then did English and French develop so differently? Largely because of Roman influence—or lack of it. In Gaul, Latin mixed with the local dialect before the Vikings added their linguistic influence; in Britain it did not. That is why French is one of the Romance languages and English is not.

death by torture, cutting off hands, and burning out eyes with hot irons—these too were part of the Norman Conquest. (In his defense, historians generally consider William a fair ruler, in the sense of justice and morality.) When it was over, England was united politically but a country totally divided socially and linguistically. The ruling classes, from king to minor village officials, were Norman and spoke French; the ruled, mostly peasants and servants, were Anglo-Saxon and spoke (Old) English.

And that condition triggered the next major change in the English language, giving us Middle English.

Like the Viking invaders before them, the Norman invaders settled permanently in England and soon thought of themselves as English. In such situations throughout history, the cultures of the invader and the invaded (and their languages) blend to form a third. To a large extent that happened in the Norman Conquest of England. Just as Old English was a mixture of Gaelic and Teutonic, *Middle English was a mixture of Old English and French*.

But the two mixed in a curious way. Because the noble classes spoke French and the peasants Anglo-Saxon, the words likely to be used in upper-class life stayed French, and those common in peasant or servant life stayed English. Through the centuries they have still not blended completely, and today we have *Oxford* and *Cockney* English. Their difference was charmingly dramatized in George Bernard Shaw's *Pygmalion*, later set to music by Alan Jay Lerner and Frederick Loewe as the popular musical comedy *My Fair Lady*. The very proper, aristocratic English of Professor Henry Higgins was Norman, and the 'orrible 'owling of Eliza Doolittle was Anglo-Saxon.

That difference, too, shows in all of us every time our emotions demand quick, strong expression. In these situations those pithy, energetic four-letter words that satisfy most of us are largely Anglo-Saxon. What determined which words are vulgar and which are acceptable in polite society? The battlefield, of course. The victors always declare themselves genteel and the vanquished to be slobs and louts. If Harold had defeated William at Hastings the slobs and louts might swear in words of French origin, and the genteel expressions might be those four-letter words that now cause the timid to blush. And why does the English-speaking world assign words of Latin origin to textbooks and relegate their exact English equivalents to pornography? Because Latin, even more than French, won its respectability on the battlefield. At two key points in the history of English, a people speaking a Latin-based language defeated and occupied a people speaking a Gaelic-based language: the Roman occupation of Gaul (creating French) and the Norman occupation of England (creating Middle English). This history also accounts for a large number of Latin-based words in the English vocabulary.

The most important writing of the Middle English period is the poetry of Geoffrey Chaucer. Then, as now, writers wrote the things readers like to read; *The Canterbury Tales* contains vivid romantic descriptions that shocked prudish readers in Chaucer's time. Although closer to today's English, the writing of Chaucer is still impossible to understand without the help of a specialist.

Modern English (1500 to present)—No military occupation, no infusion of foreign tongue at swordpoint, caused the final major change in English. Rather, the sudden shift to the English of today was triggered by a combination of social and technological shakeups.

As Europe's kings strengthened their rule and "nations" emerged, invariably the new and powerful rulers took away the lands and the armies of the old feudal lords. The end of feudalism (in the 11th and 12th centuries) was the end of the Dark Ages. But in the new kind of society that was the Middle Ages, the people most affected were the serfs: No longer could they rely on a lord to provide their basic needs. A chandler, for example, under the old system lived and worked under the protection of

take place as English passes through history. In Elizabethan England, *wherefore* was the common word for *why*. You can't possibly know that (and other changes like it) as you read Shakespeare unless someone tells you, and so you rely on a specialist (usually an English teacher). Yes, unedited Shakespeare is hard to read today; without help you will almost invariably misunderstand many passages.

This is not your fault—or Shakespeare's. He wrote for the common people *of his time*; he simply had no way of predicting the language changes that would come.

a duke who would distribute his entire output of candles as the duke saw fit, in exchange for food and lodging. Now circumstances forced the chandler to sell his candles directly to those who used them, and to buy the goods and services he needed directly from those who provided them. Commerce, unknown to Europe for a thousand years, developed. And with it, something else Europe had known much earlier: a middle class. Merchants and craftsmen emerged, and with them craft guilds, schools, and middle class participation in religion and the arts. And The Renaissance was under way.

"Renaissance" is the French word for "rebirth." But it was more than just the rebirth of the middle classes. The printing press was invented, and literacy and education expanded as books became more available. Equally important, the square-rigged sailing vessel was invented, and with it came exposure to, and influence from, other countries. The true Renaissance, then, was a rebirth of intellectual curiosity throughout Europe and England.

The English language by this time had grown used to changing at the drop of a hat (especially if the hat belonged to an invading swordsman). Adaptability, in fact, had already become a major trait of English. With the vast exposure to the languages of the Continent, English began picking up some of their stronger traits—especially in sentence structure, which until now had remained largely Teutonic (verb at the end). And in a relatively short time English underwent what linguists consider its last major change.

For all these reasons, the English language of Shakespeare (who lived early in the Modern English period) was quite different from that of authors only slightly before him. Our language continues to change. (Indeed, unedited Shakespeare is extremely hard to understand today without the help of a specialist.)

Latin's Influence—English is not one of the Romance (or Roman) languages. (They are Italian, Spanish, French, Portuguese, and Romanian.) It is of Teutonic origin and is more directly related to German, Dutch, and the Scandinavian languages. True, we have many Latin-based words. But most of them came from Roman Catholic liturgy, or from French (which is Latin-based) during the Norman Conquest, or from translators of ancient literature who had greater respect for the Classical languages than for their native English. (After all, Latin was the language of the church—and the universities.) In general, Latin has had little effect on English. Their grammatical structures are very different. Attempts to apply Latin rules to English almost always fail.

Latin grammar is in the category called *inflectional*. That is, the *endings* of words, not their positions in the sentence, tell their grammatical roles in the action being described. In the Latin-like sentence, "Dogus bit personum," the *us* ending (for subject) and *um* (for object) tell clearly which is bitor and which is bitee. The relationship of the dog and the person is the same regardless of the order of the words. In fact, any order of the words is acceptable; the meaning stays unchanged.

English grammar, on the other hand, is *syntactical*. This means the *positions* of the words in the sentence (syntax), not their endings, determines their roles in the sentence and the action it describes. "Dog bit person" and "Person bit dog" use identical words, but there can be no doubt, from their positions, who did what to whom. Furthermore, we can sense these relationships even if we have never seen or heard the words before and don't know what they mean. (For example: *Brithels glape onargs.*)

Its Characteristics

Vocabulary Is Changeable, Cosmopolitan—a hodge-podge, really. From its beginning, English has never hesitated to take useful words and grammatical traits from other languages. At first it was forced to do so by foreign armies, but the habit

---

Whose English is better?

The British generally consider American English barbaric. Most Americans concede the point without argument and consider anyone with a British accent to be a linguistic giant; we suffer a national inferiority complex about language. Should we?

There are no major differences between British and American English—except, of course, pronunciation.

Grammar

There are only two minor differences.

British say "British Leyland Motors *have* introduced *their* new . . . ." (collective nouns take plural verbs and pronouns). Americans say "General Motors *has* introduced *its* new . . . ." (collective nouns take singular verbs and pronouns).

British say "When everyone had *got* there . . . ." (*gotten* is improper). Americans say "When everyone had *gotten* there . . . ." BUT NOTE: Our pilgrim ancestors (and all other English-speaking people of the 17th century) said "When everyone had *gotten* there . . . ." Americans, then, use the form that was proper Elizabethan English.

Vocabulary

In formal usage, few words change. (One interesting exception: the "period" at the end of an American sentence is called a "full stop" in England.) Most differences are in idiom or slang: British *tubes* are American *subways*; British

stayed. It is for this reason we often have the choice of several words to express the same idea—a trait especially useful for controlling poetic rhythm. Most languages do not accept outside influence so easily. German, our first cousin, almost refuses to do so; it is quite the opposite of English in this respect.

Grammar Is Simple—Compared to most other major languages, English grammar is a joy. Our nouns and adjectives do not have gender (masculine, feminine, or neuter). Noun endings do not change for different uses. Our verbs have very few different forms. Yet, though relatively uncomplicated, the language is remarkably efficient.

Spelling And Pronunciation Are Nightmares—Here is the real madness of English. No other language is so inconsistent. By what rules do we explain "half–staff–laugh–graph," or "enough–bluff," or "ocean–motion"? Scholars don't even try.

English is Undemocratic—Because our spelling and pronunciation are so illogical, more formal education is likely to be needed than for most other languages. And English appeals to snobbish users because so many levels of vocabulary are possible. For these reasons experts generally consider it a somewhat undemocratic language.

No More Sudden Changes—Mass media tend to speed up vocabulary changes (especially in English, where change has been a fundamental trait). But mass media and mass education have slowed down changes in the *structure* of our language. It will probably never undergo sudden changes that would create a new English "period" in future centuries.

shoppers *queue up*, Americans *stand in line*; (except in New York City, where they stand *on* line); British *ring up*, Americans *telephone* (verb).

Spelling

British use: col*our,* hon*our;* Americans use: col*or*, hon*or*. British use: cent*re*, fib*re*; Americans use: cent*er*, fib*er*. British use: minim*ise*, organ*ise*; Americans use: mini*mize*, organ*ize*.

Pronunciation

Ah, here is where the British cast their spell. The American says "Half of the staff laugh at the photograph"—with the *a* as in *cat*. The Oxford scholar says "Hah-lf of the stah-ff lauh-gh at the photo-grah-ph"—with the *a* as in *far*. (But not all the English go to Oxford, and many of them sound considerably less charming.) Note, incidentally, the four different ways of spelling the *f* sound in the sentence "Half of the staff laugh at the photograph;" such inconsistencies are the same on both sides of the Atlantic, and they are more common in English than in any other major language.

Americans are usually surprised to learn that our way is the way Shakespeare and Queen Elizabeth would have pronounced those words. After crossing the Atlantic to the New World, the colonists kept (and still use) the pronunciation of the *original* mother tongue; it is the mother tongue that changed. The broad *a* (hah-lf), today the mark of the cultured, educated English, is of Cockney origin and was considered undignified until the mid-nineteenth century.

"The first human being who hurled a curse instead of a weapon against his adversary was the founder of civilization."

—*Sigmund Freud*

Ms. Archibald,

As the head of your family, I feel certain that you care about the work of some heroic educators who are fighting to protect your childrens' freedom of education.

America's schools face a serious challenge—one which could effect your children for years to come. Parents often complain when schools allow teachers to decide curriculum. This is their right, duty and privilege. Dr. Marie Zaleski, chairman of the Duncan-Pratt Committee's new legislative sub-committee first called attention to it at a public hearing last month. All of us know that every regulation, even those written by well intentioned legislators, end up doing some harm along with the good. To you and I, the challenge is to minimize that harm; but its not easy. I am proud to say that the Duncan-Pratt Committee has only been criticized once for supporting unsuccessful legislation, and took action afterward to amend it.

Since 1974, the Duncan-Pratt Committee that, for the purpose of providing support to public institutions fostering the type of legislation which is fashionably referred to in Washington as "for the public interest", however elusive and hard to define that term may be. Such legislation should always place the interests of the individual above all other interests. Americans have traditionally demanded this philosophical guideline, and are entitled to it. Now, however, a determined group of educators are trying to permanently change that.

The Committee can stop this challenge but we need your help. Not money, just a letter. We are urging every citizen to write their Congressional Representative. Just a few words will do, since your legislator is influenced more by the number of responses than by they're length. Its' urgent that you send Washington the message to vote against the Probst-Williams Bill.

Its defeat will insure freedom in our schools, protect your children, and a small but important constitutional freedom will remain protected.

       Sincerely yours,

The letter at left is worse than most real ones you are likely to see. In just 288 words, it contains the errors in grammar, punctuation, and usage most commonly made by business men and women.
Circle every error you find in the letter.
The answer key is on page 22. Then, on the two pages following, you will find *brief* explanations of the answers. With each one, the page number is given for the detailed discussion of that subject.

All mistakes are in boldface type and are numbered. The correct versions, and the explanations, are on the following two pages.

Ms. Archibald,

As the head of your family, I feel[1] certain that you care about the work of some heroic educators who are fighting to protect your **childrens'**[2] freedom of education.

America's schools face a serious challenge—one **which**[3] could **effect**[4] your children for years to come. Parents often complain when schools allow teachers to decide curriculum. **This**[5] is **their**[6] right, **duty and**[7] privilege. Dr. Marie Zaleski, **chairman**[8] of the Duncan-Pratt Committee's new legislative sub-**committee first**[9] called attention to **it**[10] at a public hearing last month. All of us know that every regulation, even **those**[11] written by **well intentioned**[12] legislators, **end**[13] up doing some harm along with the good. To **you and I,**[14] the challenge is to minimize that harm; but **its**[15] not easy. I am proud to say that the Duncan-Pratt Committee **has only been criticized once**[16] for supporting unsuccessful **legislation, and took**[17] action afterward to amend it.

Since 1974, the Duncan-Pratt **Committee that,**[18] for the purpose of providing support to public institutions fostering the type of legislation **which**[19] is fashionably referred to in Washington as "for the public **interest",**[20] however elusive and hard to define that term may be[21] Such legislation should always place the interests of the individual above all other interests. Americans have traditionally demanded this philosophical **guideline, and**[22] are entitled to it. Now, however, a determined **group of educators are**[23] trying **to permanently change that.**[24]

The Committee can stop this **challenge but**[25] we need your help. **Not money, just a letter**[26] We are urging **every citizen to write their**[27] Congressional Representative. Just a few words will do **since**[28] your legislator is influenced more by the number of responses than by **they're**[29] length. **Its'**[30] urgent that you send Washington the message to vote against the Probst-Williams Bill.

Its defeat will **insure**[31] freedom in our **schools, protect**[32] your children, and a small but important constitutional freedom will remain protected.

Sincerely yours,

Explanations

1. "*As the head of your family, I feel . . .*" says that the writer ("I") is the head of the reader's family. This is the classic DANGLING PARTICIPLE. (See "Should Participles Dangle?" page 87.)

2. The plural of *child* is *children*; its possessive is *children's*. There is no such word as *childrens*, and therefore there can be no such possessive form as *childrens'*. (See "Possessive Case," page 28.)

3. ". . . *that* could . . ." is correct here, not "*which*." (See "That vs. Which," and "The Which Hunt," page 92.)

4. ". . . *affect* . . ." is correct here, not "*effect*." (See "Commonly Misused Words," page 84.)

5. *What* is their right—to complain, or to decide curriculum? The sentence doesn't tell clearly what noun the pronoun "*This*" substitutes for. (See "Pronoun Antecedents," page 76.)

6. *Whose* right—parents, schools, or teachers? You can study the passage forever and not know. The sentence gives no indication what noun the pronoun *their* replaces. (See "Pronoun Antecedents," page 76.)

7. ". . . *right, duty, and privilege* . . ." is correct. (See "Commas," page 63.)

8. ". . . *chairwoman* of the committee . . ." would be more appropriate for Marie than *chairman*. (See "Guidelines for Nonsexist Writing," page 109.)

9. ". . . *subcommittee, first* . . ." is correct here. (See "The Missing Second Comma," page 78.)

10. Called attention to *what?* As in 5 and 6, the sentence provides no noun that allows the reader to know what the pronoun means. (In this case the pronoun is *it*.) Readers might not notice an error of this kind; they would simply be unaware they had received some imprecise information. (See "Pronoun Antecedents," page 76.)

11. ". . . even *one* written by . . ." is correct here, not "*those*," (because *regulation* is singular). (See "Noun and Pronoun Must Agree," page 75.)

12. "*Well-intentioned* . . . " should be hyphenated (because it's a compound adjective). (See "The Elegant Punctuation Marks," page 66.)

13. ". . . *ends* up doing . . ." is correct here, not "*end*," (because *regulation* is singular. (See "Subject and Verb Must Agree," page 75.)

14. "To you and *me* . . ." is correct, Not "*I*." (See "The Case for Pronouns," page 77.)

15. ". . . but *it's* not . . ." is correct here, not "*its*." (See "Commonly Misused Words," page 86.)

16. ". . . has been criticized *only* once . . ." is correct here, not "has *only* been criticized once." (See "The Wandering Only," page 52.)

17. "... *legislation and took* ..." is correct here, or "... *legislation, and we took* ..." if you wish. (See "The Noble English Sentence," page 48; "Commas," page 62.)

The next four errors are part of a terrible sentence. In fact, it's not a sentence but a carelessly assembled collection of words making little sense. We all see examples such as this in real life occasionally; we laugh at or scorn the people who write them.

18. "... Committee, *which* ..." is correct here, not "Committee *that.*" (See "Non-restrictive Clauses," page 39.)

19. "... legislation *that* ..." is correct here, not "*which.*" (See "That vs. Which," page 92.)

20. A small point: commas should always go *inside* quotation marks when the two are used together. So should periods. Therefore, " ... *for the public interest,*" is correct. (See page 64.)

21. HUH? Surely this is not the end of the sentence. Everything from *Committee* (the subject) to the period is just a hodge-podge. It's not a clause (because it doesn't have a subject and predicate) or a phrase (because it doesn't serve collectively as one of the parts of speech.) It just hangs there, making the reader wonder when and how the sentence will end. Readers who care enough to study it carefully learn it doesn't end; the subject doesn't have a verb. Writers who try complicated sentences often create this kind of embarrassment. (See "Phrases," page 37; "Clauses," page 38; "Sentences," page 48; "About Sentence Fragments," page 50.)

22. "... *guideline and are* ..." is correct, or "... guideline, and *they* are ..." if you wish. (See "Sentences," page 48; "Commas," page 62.)

23. "... group of educators *is* ..." is correct here, not "*are.*" (See "Subject and Verb Must Agree," page 75.)

24. "... *to change that permanently* ..." gets rid of the split infinitive. (See "Should You Split an Infinitive?" page 40.)

25. "... *this challenge, but we need* ..." is correct here. (See "Clauses," page 38; "Sentences," page 48; "Commas," page 62.)

26. Well, this is not so bad. But it is a sentence fragment, not a complete sentence. (See "About Sentence Fragments," page 50.)

27. "... every citizen to write *his or her* ... Representative" or "... *all citizens* to write *their* ..." would be correct here. (See "Noun and Pronoun Must Agree," page 75; "Guidelines for Nonsexist Writing," page 108.)

28. "... *because* your legislator ..." is correct here, not "*since.*" (See "Commonly Misused Words," page 84.)

29. "... by *their* length ..." is correct here, not "*they're.*" (See "Commonly Misused Words," page 88.)

30. "*It's* urgent that ..." is correct here; there is no such word as *its'.* (See "Commonly Misused Words," page 86.)

31. " ... *ensure* ... " is correct here, not "*insure.*" (See "Commonly Misused Words," page 85.)

32. " ... *schools and protect* ..." is correct here, because the three items connected by commas are not a true series; the comma after "*children*" then makes this an ordinary compound sentence. (See "False Series," page 77; "Compound Sentences," page 49.)

Words:
The Parts of Speech

(There Are Only Eight, and You Really Must Learn Them)

Words: The Parts of Speech

(There Are Only Eight, and You Really Must Learn Them)

THE KEY WORDS ARE: Adjective, adverb, conjunction (or connective), interjection, noun, preposition, pronoun, and verb. BUT: The same word can serve as different parts of speech. *Following*, for example, can be a noun (They have a large *following*), verb (We are *following* you), adjective (The *following* day), or preposition (*Following* the election). The part of speech of a word depends on how it is used in the sentence containing it.

What's All The Fuss About 'Modifiers'?

You can't avoid them if you're going to use grammar correctly. Modifiers add some meaning—usually important—to the words they modify, making them more exact. **THERE ARE ONLY TWO KINDS: ADJECTIVES AND ADVERBS.**

> *newest* computers (adjective)   speak *clearly* (adverb)

To appreciate the importance of modifiers, consider the sentence: *Pipelines carry oil*. (This sentence structure, incidentally, is the backbone of the English language: subject, transitive verb, direct object. See "The Noble English Sentence," page 48.)

Well, *Pipelines carry oil* is not a very exciting sentence. More important, it's not very accurate. *Some* (adjective) *pipelines carry oil* tells more. *Some pipelines carry oil inefficiently* (adverb) is an entirely different statement. The modifiers *some* and *inefficiently* make the difference.

As you'll see in the next chapter, phrases and clauses also serve as modifiers—but, like single words, always as adjectives or adverbs.

ADJECTIVE. **Modifies or adds to a noun or pronoun by describing or limiting its meaning in your writing (*favorable* decision; *predicted* volume; *large* ones).** Several adjectives may modify the same noun (*the brilliant, efficient, new sales* representative). Note, however, that adjectives are not always found next to the noun they modify (the new sales rep has proved to be *brilliant* . . .). *A, an*, and *the* are the most commonly used adjectives. They are *articles*. (See *Other Grammar Terms*, page 118.)

ADVERB. **Modifies or adds to a verb (*ad verb*) by telling WHEN (*suddenly* realized), WHERE (arriving *there*), HOW (trying *desperately*), or WHY (We waited *because* . . . .).** May also modify an adjective (*badly* damaged merchandise), or another adverb (*very highly* trained). Adverbs usually end with '-ly' (*easily*), but not always (soon). Like adjectives, several may modify the same word, and they are not necessarily next to the word they modify.

CONJUNCTION. **Also called 'connective.' Connects words or complete ideas.** These little words are more important than most writers realize because they *bridge* your ideas; they help the reader *see* some relationship you, the writer, can *feel*. There are three kinds: (1) **Coordinate C's** (and, but, or, nor, for, so, yet. The chairman *and* the president; I gathered the data, *but* she wrote the report) connect two independent clauses. (2) **Subordinate C's** (although, as, because, if, unless, etc.) connect a phrase or subordinate clause to a main clause by showing some relationship between them: (*If* you go, don't come back; There have been fewer errors *since* the change). (3) **Correlative C's** (Either-or, neither-nor, whether-or, both-and, not only-but) connect pairs and must always appear in the sentence as pairs. Conjunctions are little gems in building your logic.

CONNECTIVE. **A more modern word for 'conjunction.'**

INTERJECTION. **An exclamation, usually at the beginning of a sentence, serving no grammatical function (*Oh*, that's not true; *Well*, I see you're late again).** It may be a sentence of its own requiring neither subject nor verb (*For goodness sake!*). Interjections usually express emotion.

NOUN. **The name for a thing (*computer*), idea (*truth*), process (*manufacturing*), or condition (*illness*). Nouns always serve as the subject of a clause, or as an object.** In many languages, the form or ending of the noun changes to show its grammatical function. In English it does not; the function a noun serves is shown by its position in the sentence (Person bit dog; dog bit person). Largely for this reason, grammar is simpler in English than in most other major languages. (That may surprise you, but it's true.) In languages which do use changing noun forms to show function, these forms are called 'declensions.' *Proper Nouns* are the capitalized names of people, places, organizations, and products. Adding *s* or *es* to most nouns makes them plural. (Exceptions: Nouns ending with *y* use *ies* for the plural. [These, too, have exceptions: *attorney/attorneys*.] There are also some irregular nouns, such as *man/men, mouse/mice*.) Adding *'s* to most nouns makes them possessive.

Nouns and verbs are the most basic parts of speech. If you can't tell them apart, keep studying and practicing until you can.

PREPOSITION. **Connects a noun (or word functioning as a noun) with some other part of the same sentence.** Usually, it describes place (*on* the desk; *to* our office) or time (*before* the audit *in* 1984), but not always (*for, with*, etc.).

PRONOUN. **Substitutes for a noun (*pro noun*), or for a phrase or clause serving as a noun (*He* mailed *it* to *them*).** There are eight kinds: (1) **Personal P's,** which may stand for first person (I, we), second person (you), or third person (he, she,

I feel GOOD
or
I feel WELL?

If you're talking about your health, *good* is correct.

You feel *well* (adverb) only when you're talking about the efficiency with which you feel something.

A misunderstanding that had to happen

If some of Shakespeare's language (early modern English) is hard to understand today, Chaucer (middle English) is even harder and the language of *Beowulf* (early English) impossible. Throughout the history of English, then, the greatest literature has been challenging to read.

Gradually, as a result, it was almost inevitable the attitude would develop (especially among the educated): *Good writing has always been hard to understand; therefore, so should mine be.* That's a fairly common attitude among people who are not trained as writers but must write anyhow. "*Make it as complex as possible*" seems their battle cry.

Such people have missed an important point: *Shakespeare's writing was NOT hard to understand at the time he wrote it. It is today, simply because the language has changed so much since then.*

So often it's the WRITING STYLE, not the CONTENT, that gives the readers trouble. That's certainly true of early literature—for reasons easy to explain. But it would be impossible to justify *today* writing deliberately in a style that's hard to understand—unless you want deliberately to be unclear or are trying to impress others with your language skills. A more sensible attitude: impress with your IDEAS, not the WORDS AND SENTENCES used to convey them. Indeed, the more complex the ideas, the greater the need to express them in clear, simple language so people can understand them fully (and be impressed by your *thinking*).

it, or they). (2) **Relative P's** (who, which, that, etc.), which relate a subordinate part of a sentence to the main clause (as here). (3) **Demonstrative P's** (this, that, these, those), which point out a specific person or thing. (4) **Indefinite P's,** which refer to people or things generally rather than specifically (all, some, etc.). (5) **Interrogative P's,** which ask a question (who, what, which, etc.). They may be the same words as Relative Pronouns (of subordinate clauses), but they are part of the main clause (*Which* regulation is the most recent?). (6) **Numerical P's,** which are numbers standing for nouns (The *second* was the least important *one*). (7) **Reflexive P's,** which are formed by adding '-self' or '-selves' to a personal pronoun. (8) **Reciprocal P's,** which stand for two or more people or things interacting; the verb tells the interaction between them (These rulings contradict *each other*). NOW, IMPRESS FRIENDS BY RECITING THOSE AT A COCKTAIL PARTY.

In English, the form of the pronoun usually (but not always) changes to describe three other things about the noun it stands for: *Number*, which tells whether the noun is singular or plural (I, we); *Sex* (gender), which tells whether the noun is masculine, feminine, or neuter (he, she, it); and *Case*, which tells whether the noun is the subject of the verb (nominative case), object of a verb or preposition (objective case), or possessor of another noun (possessive case). Example of all three: *He* (nominative) said that *your* (possessive) duties would be shared by *me* (objective).

As with nouns, the various forms of pronouns that show different relationships are called 'declensions.'

VERB. The action word. Every sentence or clause must contain at least one. It tells what the subject (a noun or pronoun) is or does. The verb may be transitive (requiring an object), intransitive (complete without an object), or linking (requiring more information). Examples: **Transitive:** Perkins (subject) collects (transitive verb) coins (direct object). **Intransitive:** She (subject) snores (complete verb). **Linking:** Geldings (subject) are (linking verb) neutered male (predicate adjectives) horses (predicate nominative). A simple test to tell whether a word is a verb: Ask yourself, "*Can it be done?*" Be sure, without fail, to read our comments on *predicate adjective* and *predicate nominative*, page 122.

In English, the form of the verb usually (but not always) changes to tell five other things about the action it describes: (1) **Number,** which tells whether the subject is singular or plural (It *turns*; they *turn*). (2) **Person,** which tells whether the subject is I, you, he, she, it, or they (I *am*; you *are*; he, she, or it *is*; they *are*). (3) **Tense,** which tells whether the action is in the past, present, or future (*reviewed, review, will review*). (4) **Voice,** which tells whether the subject performs the action (active) or receives it (passive). (The IBM representative *gathered* [active voice] the information; The information *was gathered* [passive voice] by the IBM representative). (5) **Mood,** which tells whether the action is fact (indicative mood, the most commonly used), command (imperative mood), or contrary to fact (subjunctive mood). (You *are* here; *Be* here; If you *were* here . . .). These varying forms of verb are called its 'conjugations.'

Verbs and nouns are the two most basic parts of speech. As you already know because you read the section on nouns (page 27), if you can't tell them apart, keep studying and practicing until you can.

Do You Really Know the Eight Parts of Speech?

Self-Study Exercise

If you haven't read "The Parts of Speech" (pages 26 through 28), you don't belong here; do yourself a favor and take the time to go back and read them. Even if you feel certain about them, the brush-up will help. And if you really know them it will be easy. These eight kinds of words, and the differences between them, are so basic you must know them. Here are some examples, followed by self-tests.

ADJECTIVE (modifies nouns or pronouns)
lean, juicy meat (*lean* and *juicy* tell more about the noun *meat*)
loud music (*loud* tells more about the noun *music*)
two new ones (*two* and *new* tell more about the pronoun *ones*)

ADVERB (modifies verbs, adjectives, or other adverbs)
arrived *late* (*late* tells more about the verb *arrived*)
perfectly adjusted instrument (*perfectly* tells more about the adjective *adjusted*, which tells more about the noun *instrument*). BUT WAIT! Isn't *adjusted* a verb? Normally yes, and if your intuition told you that, you've got good intuition—simply wrong this time. In this case, *adjusted* modifies a noun (instrument), so it's an adjective.
very slowly (*very* tells more about the adverb *slowly*)

CONJUNCTION (also called 'connective,' connects words or ideas)
labor *and* management (coordinate c)
if prices come down (subordinate c)
whether you go *or* not (correlative c—always in pairs)

INTERJECTION (short, emotional statement)
Wow, this job is difficult!

NOUN (the name of something, always a subject or object)
Our *report* (subject) is ready.
They wear special *uniforms* (direct object).
on the other *side* of the computer *printout* (indirect objects [of prepositions])
BUT WAIT! Isn't *computer* a noun? Again, good (but wrong) instincts. Normally a noun, *computer* here modifies the noun *printout*, so it's an adjective.

PREPOSITION (connects a noun with another idea—usually in time or place)
with our help
at the plans
by the customer
(These are all prepositional phrases.)

PRONOUN (stands for a noun, hence its name; that noun is its 'antecedent')
listening to *her* (personal p)
which arrived late (relative p)
(These are the most common, but there are others: see page 27.)

VERB (the action word of a sentence)
Cyd *hates* (transitive verb, present tense, active voice) martinis.
The parts *will be shipped* (future tense, passive voice) tomorrow.
Your request *was* (past tense, linking) unreasonable.

Self-Study Exercises

(Answer Key: pages 32 and 33)

A SPECIAL MESSAGE: If you feel you can gain the help you need by answering the questions in your mind, without writing the answers:

No, you can't!

Exercise 1:

Each of the two eight-word sentences below contains all eight parts of speech. You should be able to identify each word:

Oh, and after several attempts they finally succeeded.

Oh (_____), and (_____) after

(_____) several (_____) attempts

(_____) they (_____) finally

(_____) succeeded (_____).

Wow, but I object strongly to computer games.

Wow (_____), but (_____) I

(_____) object (_____) strongly

(_____) to (_____) computer

(_____) games (_____).

Exercise 2:

Identify the part of speech of each of the italicized words:

2-1. replaced *its* engine (_____)

2-2. the basketball *team* (_____)

2-3. *in* the warehouse (_____)

2-4. our *best* opportunity (_____)

2-5. *close* the door (_____)

2-6. cans *and* bottles (_____)

2-7. *Oh*, I thought (_____)

2-8. you *definitely* said (_____)

2-9. yes, *but* they will (_____)

2-10. it *is* not necessary (_____)

2-11. looking *at* the plans (_____)

2-12. the *extra* point (_____)

2-13. *Listen*, you guys are (_____)

2-14. seventy-six *trombones* (_____)

30

2-15. how *well* you know them (_____)

2-16. the one *that* got away (_____)

Exercise 3:

Some words are formed from one part of speech but may be used as another. Remember, it's how a word is used in a particular sentence that determines its part of speech in that sentence. Now try these; they'll be harder:

3-1. The *flying* nun now uses a helicopter. (_____)

3-2. See *if* the drawing has arrived. (_____)

3-3. *Flying* is the safest way to travel. (_____)

3-4. This plan is *impossible* to understand. (_____)

3-5. *Well*, the judge said the decision was unfair. (_____)

3-6. It was the ratings *that* impressed her most. (_____)

3-7. They need more light *above* the controls. (_____)

3-8. I know, *however*, some of you disagree. (_____)

3-9. We succeeded on our second *try*. (_____)

3-10. The *above* statement is incomplete. (_____)

3-11. *Try* to remember what she told you. (_____)

3-12. They're performing *well* today. (_____)

NOW COMPARE YOUR ANSWERS with the answer key, pages 32 and 33. Pat yourself on the back (briefly) for correct answers, then study the INCORRECT ones. *They are your learning opportunities.* For each wrong answer, go back to the page in the text (listed in the answer key) and re-read the explanation until you understand your error. *Remember, your mistakes are your opportunity to improve. THEY ARE THE REASON YOU ARE READING THIS BOOK.*

YOU WILL BE ASKED SIMILAR QUESTIONS in the next section, on phrases and clauses. Identifying the parts of speech for *groups of words*, though based on exactly the same principles, will be more difficult than for the individual words you have just finished.

Exercise 1:

Oh, and after several attempts they finally succeeded.

Oh (*interjection*), and (*conjunction*) after (*preposition*) several (*adjective*) attempts (*noun*) they (*pronoun*) finally (*adverb*) succeeded (*verb*).

Wow, but I object strongly to computer games.

Wow (*interjection*), but (*conjunction*) I (*pronoun*) object (*verb*) strongly (*adverb*) to (*preposition*) computer (*adjective*) games (*noun*).

IF YOU MISSED ANY OF THESE, OR IF YOU FELT UNSURE WHILE ANSWERING, DO YOURSELF A FAVOR AND REREAD THE DEFINITIONS OF THE EIGHT PARTS OF SPEECH (pages 26-29). DOING SO WILL TAKE ONLY A FEW MINUTES AND WILL HELP YOU BUILD A SOLID UNDERSTANDING OF ALL THAT FOLLOWS.

Exercise 2:

2-1. replaced *its* engine . . . (*pronoun*) Possessive. Page 28.

2-2. the basketball *team* . . . (*noun*) A thing. Page 27.

2-3. *in* the warehouse . . . (*preposition*) Connects a noun with something. Page 27.

2-4. our *best* opportunity . . . (*adjective*) Modifies 'opportunity.' Page 27.

2-5. *close* the door . . . (*verb*) Action. Page 28.

2-6. cans *and* bottles . . . (*conjunction*) Bridges or connects two ideas. Page 27.

2-7. *Oh*, I thought . . . (*interjection*) An exclamation. Page 27.

2-8. you *definitely* said . . . (*adverb*) Modifies 'said.' Page 27.

2-9. yes, *but* they will . . . (*conjunction*) Bridges or connects two ideas. Page 27.

2-10. it *is* not necessary . . . (*verb*) Action. Page 28.

2-11. looking *at* the plans . . . (*preposition*) Connects a noun with something. Page 27.

2-12. the *extra* point . . . (*adjective*) Modifies 'point.' Page 27.

2-13. *Listen*, you guys are . . . (*interjection*) Normally a verb, here an exclamation. Page 27.

2-14. seventy-six *trombones* . . . (*noun*) Things. Page 27.

2-15. how *well* you know them . . . (*adverb*) Modifies 'know.' Page 27.

2-16. the one *that* got away . . . (*pronoun*) Relative. Page 28.

Exercise 3:

3-1. The *flying* nun . . . (*adjective*). Generally a verb, here a participle (adjective). Page 27.

3-2. See *if* the drawing . . . (*conjunction*). It subordinates one idea to another. Page 27.

3-3. *Flying* is the safest . . . (*noun*). Generally a verb, here it's a gerund (subject). Page 27.

3-4. This plan is *impossible* . . . (*adjective*). Modifies the noun 'plan.' Page 27.

3-5. *Well*, the judge . . . (*interjection*). An exclamation; it adds nothing to the meaning. Page 27.

3-6. ratings *that* impressed her . . . (*pronoun*). Relative. Page 27.

3-7. *above* the controls . . . (*preposition*). Connects a noun with something. Page 27.

3-8. I know, *however*, some . . . (*adverb*). Used here as a conjunction. Page 27.

3-9. on our second *try* . . . (*noun*). A thing. Page 27.

3-10. The *above* statement . . . (*adjective*). Modifies the noun 'statement.' Page 27.

3-11. *Try* to remember . . . (*verb*). Action. Page 28.

3-12. They're performing *well* . . . (*adverb*). Modifies the verb 'performing.' Page 27.

Answer Key
to pages 30
and 31

Talk about embedding!

(See page 52.)

Of all the fleas that ever flew
(And flying fleas are rather few
((Because for proper flying you
(((Whether you are a flea or not)))
Need wings and things fleas have not got)))—

(I make the further point that fleas
Are thick as these parentheses
((An illustration (((you'll agree)))
Both apt and pleasing to a flea)))—

Now then where were we? Let me see—
Ah, yes—We said to fly you ought
(Whether you are a flea or not)
To have some wings (yes, at least two
((At least no less than two will do
(((And fleas have something less than one
((((One less, in fact (((((or, frankly, none,
Which ((((((as once more you will agree))))))
Limits the flying of a flea))))))))))))))).

And let me add that fleas that fly
Are known as Flears. (You can see why.)
All I have said thus far is true.
(If it's not clear, that's up to you.
((You'll have to learn sometime, my dear,
That what is true may not be clear
(((While what is clear may not be true
((((And you'll be wiser when you do.))))))))))

—Saturday Review

Phrases and Clauses: Building Words into Ideas

Phrases and Clauses: Building Words into Ideas

THE KEY WORDS ARE: Phrase, clause, restrictive, nonrestrictive, dependent, independent, appositive.

An ongoing controversy

In 1974 the Conference of College Composition and Communication, a branch of the National Council of Teachers of English, issued the following policy statement:

"We affirm the students' right to their own patterns and varieties of language— the dialects of their nurture or whatever dialects in which they find their own identity and style."

The well-meaning educators could hardly have issued a more damaging statement if they were racists and bigots, for the surest way to lock minority students into the ghetto— and out of mainstream USA—is to let them leave our schools and

These two statements contain exactly the same information:

> Kovall, traded to the Brewers by the Red Sox in 1982, was American League rookie of the year in 1979, when he batted .294 with 23 home runs and 91 runs batted in, but he suffered a spinal disk injury his second year and has seen little duty since.

> Kovall was traded to the Brewers. The Red Sox traded him. The year was 1982. Earlier he had been rookie of the year. That was in the American League. The year was 1979. He batted .294 then. He also hit 23 home runs. He also batted in 91 runs. But he suffered an injury. It was to a spinal disk. This happened his second year. He has seen little duty since.

The difference between those two passages is the use of phrases and clauses. They make the first passage seem reasonable and readable, causing the ideas to flow in a smooth, easy way from the writer to the reader. In the second passage there are none but bare essential clauses, and these contain only a few modifying phrases (it would be impossible to write without any); as a result the ideas seem child-like and the flow awkward.

> BUT NOTE: Stylish writers would argue that the first passage (above) contains too much information for one sentence, and they are right. Though it is vastly better than the child-like second passage, it would be still better as two sentences. We can make a dramatic improvement simply by changing *"batted in, but . . . "* to *"batted in. But . . . ."* (Yes, you may end sentences with prepositions or begin them with conjunctions; see pages 96 through 98.) The related but separate ideas are now easier to read. Equally important, they both gain added emphasis. Dividing your ideas properly into sentences is one of the most important skills in writing. (See pages 48 through 52.)

YOU HAVE BEEN USING PHRASES AND CLAUSES ALL YOUR LIFE, or at least since early childhood, whether you know it or not. Probably you use them intuitively, and so their correct usage cannot be too difficult—in most cases. But intuition is not always correct. Being able to recognize these groups of words and understanding what they do will help you to write easily, accurately, and, if you wish, elegantly.

These subjects may have been distasteful to you earlier in life, in that period when you hated brussel sprouts because kids are supposed to. Phrases and clauses are not particularly hard to understand, however, and you really must know them if you are to use English correctly. For example, by singling them out you will be able to recognize the subject, object, and verb of a sentence you are writing—and avoid confusion (and embarrassment) by making sure they agree with each other. Also, seeing your phrases and clauses will help you to put commas where they belong (and avoid them where they don't belong).

A Phrase Is . . .

. . . a group of words working together. Not just any cluster of two or more, however; words become a phrase when they serve collectively as one of the parts of speech and when the group does not contain a *subject and verb*. It can contain a subject *or* verb, or neither, but it cannot contain both. (If it contains a subject and verb it is a clause.)

This is not nearly as complicated as it sounds. Phrases are usually a few words serving as a NOUN (You can fool *most of the people*), VERB (We *have been working* all night), ADJECTIVE (The *large and heavy* machinery), or ADVERB (We failed, *like those before us*). But some can be quite long: *During the years between Richard Nixon's humiliating political defeat in the California congressional election and the stunning victory of his election as President of the United States*, his career took . . . .

Two things cause confusion about phrases. First, a phrase can contain other phrases. The long one about Richard Nixon in the paragraph above is all one phrase, serving as an adverb modifying the verb *took*. (The phrase tells *when*). Yet it contains seven smaller embedded phrases, and these in turn can be recombined to create many others. This point can be shown more clearly with a shorter phrase: *During his presidency*, John F. Kennedy was . . . *During his presidency* is one phrase, modifying the verb *was*. (The phrase tells *when*.) But within it, *his presidency* is also a phrase—in this case serving as a noun, the object of the preposition *during*. So, phrases can overlap.

And second, the most common phrases and the ones most mentioned, prepositional phrases, do not really exist. Well, let's put that another way. Of course they exist—but as something else. Countless phrases begin with prepositions, and these are loosely called prepositional phrases. (They usually, but not always, end with a noun or pronoun.) But they never serve as prepositions. A prepositional phrase always serves as an adjective or adverb. ADJECTIVES (modifying nouns or pronouns): It's the house *on the corner* (tells what house). Investments *in real estate* are usually good tax shelters (tells what investments). Those containers *under the lights* need shields (further describes containers). ADVERBS (modifying verbs): *In 1982*, Congress reacted *quickly* (tells when they reacted). Birds fly *over the rainbow* (tells where they fly). We approved *with reluctance* (tells how we approved).

Nonrestrictive or Restrictive

(You must know this, for proper punctuation.)

A phrase is NONRESTRICTIVE if the thought it expresses does not change the basic meaning of the sentence containing it. (The grandfather clock, *at the top of the stairs*, needs to be wound.) There is one grandfather clock, and it needs to be wound; by the way, it's at the top of the stairs. (The phrase here is prepositional, serving as an adjective because it modifies the noun *clock*.) The phrase does not restrict the main idea. If you remove it, the main idea remains the same. **NOTE that nonrestrictive phrases are surrounded by commas.** Always use two commas, unless the phrase begins or ends the sentence. (All of the advice in this paragraph applies also to *clauses*, in the next section.)

A phrase is RESTRICTIVE if the thought it expresses limits (restricts), or adds to, or changes the meaning of the sentence containing it. (The grandfather clock *at the top of the stairs* needs to be wound.) There are two or more grandfather clocks, and one needs to be wound; it's the one at the top of the stairs. (The phrase here, like the nonrestrictive one in the paragraph above, is prepositional/adjectival.) This phrase definitely *restricts* the main idea described here; if you remove it, the intended meaning becomes incomplete. **NOTE that restrictive phrases are *not* separated from the rest of the sentence by commas.** (As with nonrestrictive phrases, the advice in this paragraph applies also to *clauses*, in the next section.)

colleges thinking that they don't need standard English—that "the dialects of their nurture" are enough.

Were the educators saying students may keep their ethnic dialects provided they learn to read, write, and speak standard English as well? No one needs permission for that, and the statement says nothing to encourage the study of standard English. (In fact, it goes on to deny " . . . *that the myth of a standard American dialect has any validity.*")

Most minority leaders feel strongly that minority children MUST learn the language of the society in which they hope to share a slice of the pie, and that one of the most solemn obligations of our education system is to see that they learn it.

A Clause Is . . .

. . . a group of words that has a subject (noun or pronoun) and a verb acting with that subject. It may be a whole sentence (*They arrived.*) or part of a sentence (*When they arrived,*).

A clause differs from a phrase in two ways. First, a phrase does not have both a subject and verb; a clause *must* have both. And second, a phrase always serves as some part of speech in the sentence containing it (noun, verb, adjective, or adverb); a clause may or may not. This will become clear in the next few paragraphs.

Every sentence must have at least one clause: its main clause. Some sentences have nothing else. (*Your order was shipped yesterday.*)

Independent or Dependent

An INDEPENDENT clause is one that can stand alone; as its name implies, it does not depend on the rest of the sentence to make sense. (*Smedley is going to Toronto.*) Every sentence must have a main clause, and it is always an independent clause.

> BUT NOTE: Although the basic clause is usually formed by just a few words, an independent clause need not be short. Any number of embellishments can be added through phrases and other modifiers, and, therefore, the whole statement conveyed by one clause can end up quite long. (*Because of the rush, and the long delay obtaining customs clearance by mail, Smedley is going to Toronto and will discuss the changes with the client.*) You should be able to recognize, by brushing aside the many phrases, that "Smedley is going to Toronto" is still the only clause. *Because of the rush* has no subject or verb; neither have *and the long delay, by mail*, nor *with the client. Obtaining customs clearance* has a subject (obtaining) but no verb; *and will discuss the changes* has a verb (will discuss) but no subject.

You can add one independent clause to another, stretching out a sentence: (Smedley is going to Toronto, *and the client has informed us the changes are ready.*) You can even embed one independent clause within another: (Smedley, *it was decided yesterday*, is going to Toronto.)

> BUT NOTE: Stylish writers warn against very much of that kind of embedding. It quickly becomes clumsy, hard to understand, too much for one sentence. (See pages 50 through 52.)

NOW EXAMINE this clause: (*Although Smedley is going to Toronto,*). Now the clause is no longer independent; it doesn't make sense alone. It is DEPENDENT; it depends on something else to give it sense, and that something else must be another clause. (Any way you try it, a phrase won't do.) Another subject and verb are needed. (Although Smedley is going to Toronto, *her work (subject) must not fall (verb) behind.* Now, the second one is the independent or main clause. *Her work must not fall behind* can stand alone and make sense; *Although Smedley is going to Toronto* can't.

Your writing may contain scores of dependent clauses *that simply don't contain enough information to stand alone and make sense* (such as that one). A shorter one: People *who live in glass houses* shouldn't throw stones.

You can add any number of dependent clauses to a main clause, stretching out a sentence. You can even embed one dependent clause within another: (Although Smedley is going to Toronto, her work, *because it has an early deadline*, must not fall behind.)

> BUT NOTE: As with independent clauses, stylish writers warn against very much of that kind of embedding. It quickly becomes clumsy, hard to understand, too much for one sentence. (See pages 50 through 52.)

Another name for dependent clauses is SUBORDINATE clauses. By its nature, the main (independent) clause usually contains the major idea of the sentence; the idea conveyed in the dependent clause, then, by comparison seems less important—or subordinated—to the reader. (See "Syntax," pages 50 through 52.)

Nonrestrictive or Restrictive (again)

Dependent clauses are further broken down into subcategories: NONRESTRICTIVE and RESTRICTIVE. This explanation will sound very much like that for phrases (see page 37), because the conditions are the same.

A dependent or subordinate clause is NONRESTRICTIVE if the thought it expresses does *not* change the meaning of the main clause. Its thought isn't essential to the main thought and could be omitted. (The third couple, *who ordered fish*, won the prize.) The third couple won the prize; by the way, they ordered fish. **NOTE that nonrestrictive clauses are surrounded by commas.** Always use two commas, unless the clause begins or ends the sentence.

A subordinate clause is RESTRICTIVE if the thought it expresses limits (restricts) or adds to the meaning of the main clause. If you omit it you change the meaning. (The third couple *who ordered fish* won the prize.) Many couples were there, and some of them ordered fish; the third couple who ordered fish may have been the tenth couple there, but they won the prize. **NOTE that restrictive clauses are *not* set off from the rest by commas.** (But see "Introductory Clauses," page 63.)

BE SURE to punctuate every clause correctly, to let your reader know whether its information is nonrestrictive or restrictive. There's a vast difference between:

> *Sales representatives who don't come prepared to answer your questions are a nuisance.*

> and

> *Sales representatives, who don't come prepared to answer your questions, are a nuisance.*

BY THE WAY, we said earlier that a clause may or may not serve as a part of speech in the sentence containing it. (A phrase always does.) Let's clarify. An independent (main) clause, because it can stand alone and make complete sense, could not possibly serve as one part of speech. A dependent (subordinate) clause can—in fact, always does. Every dependent clause—whether nonrestrictive or restrictive—serves as an adjective, adverb, or noun. You can see this clearly by finding the word it modifies *in the main clause*. Remember, adjectives modify nouns or pronouns; adverbs modify verbs, adjectives, or other adverbs. (Noun clauses are a little different; they may serve as the subject of the main clause, or as the object of a verb or preposition in the main clause. In that usage the dependent clause is actually part of the main clause.)

STOP HERE IF YOU'RE CONFUSED. READ SLOWLY—SEVERAL TIMES, IF YOU MUST.
THE FOLLOWING EXAMPLES SHOULD CLARIFY:

CLAUSES USED AS ADJECTIVES:
Robots *that will think more objectively than people* worry some scientists and sociologists.
(The subject of the *dependent clause* is "that"; its verb is "will think"; the clause serves as an adjective because it modifies the noun "robots" in the main clause.)

San Antonio is a city *everyone enjoys*.
(The subject of the *dependent clause* is "everyone"; its verb is

Should you split an infinitive?

Well, not usually. The infinitive is the *to* form of a verb (*to examine*); you split it by putting another word between *to* and the rest of the verb (to *carefully* examine). You can almost always unsplit it easily by just switching two words (to examine *carefully*). And when you can do this, you should.

Occasionally, however, unsplitting may create awkwardness (to *really* understand differential equations). In such cases, but *only* in such cases, even the strictest grammarians will concede that a split infinitive may be useful. Only klutzes leave infinitives split when they could unsplit them easily.

"enjoys"; the clause serves as an adjective because it modifies the noun "city" in the main clause.)

Those *who attended the meeting* said it was a waste of time. (The subject of the *dependent clause* is "who"; its verb is "attended"; the clause serves as an adjective because it modifies the pronoun "those" in the main clause.)

NOTE that adjective clauses can come in the middle of sentences or at the end, but never at the beginning.

CLAUSES USED AS ADVERBS: *After we had talked with several employees*, we decided to change the system entirely. (The subject of the *dependent clause* is "we"; its verb is "had talked"; the clause serves as an adverb because it modifies the verb "decided" in the main clause.)

The word processing system saves more time *than the purchasing department estimated*. (The subject of the *dependent clause* is "department"; its verb is "estimated"; the clause serves as an adverb because it modifies the adjective "more," which in turn modifies the noun "time," in the main clause.)

Smedley hits the ball harder *than it has ever been hit before*. (The subject of the *dependent clause* is "it"; the verb is "has been hit"; the clause serves as an adverb because it modifies the adverb "harder," which in turn modifies the verb "hits," in the main clause.)

AS NOUNS: *Whoever takes the order* must write up the paperwork. (The *dependent clause* serves as a noun because it is the subject of the main clause.)

We have no way of knowing *how customers will react* until we try selling it. (The *dependent clause* serves as a noun because it is the direct object of the verb "knowing" in the main clause.)

Free parking is available for *anyone who needs it*. (The *dependent clause* serves as a noun because it is the object of the preposition "for" in the main clause.)

An Appositive Is . . .

. . . a tricky little word or group of words placed next to a noun to identify it or express it another way. Like phrases and clauses, appositives can be NON-RESTRICTIVE (Jacques Cousteau, the famous oceanographer, has called world attention to the danger of water pollution) or RESTRICTIVE (The famous microbiologist Wolf Vishniac developed instruments to find life on Mars).

Appositives look like phrases, at first glance, in that they are groups of words. Remember, however, that a phrase always serves as some part of speech in the clause containing it; an appositive does not, and that's how you tell them apart.

Be sure to use the same punctuation rule for appositives as for phrases and clauses: commas before and after nonrestrictive; none for restrictive.

> **OVERCONFIDENCE DOESN'T PAY.** Do yourself a favor and don't try to do these exercises in your head. Write your answers in the space provided. You will learn more when you can *see* your answers and compare them with the explanations in the answer key.

Exercise 4:

Next to each of the following sentences, mark whether the italicized passage is a phrase, clause, or appositive:

4-1. Michael Spinks, *Leon's brother*, is also a boxer. _____

4-2. Who wouldn't be enticed by a dinner *at LeCoq au Vin*? _____

4-3. *Only a handful* of us stayed to the end. _____

4-4. *Because we stayed*, however, we can now operate the equipment properly. _____

4-5. *After the long and exhausting flight to Hong Kong,* we had no chance to rest before the meeting. _____

4-6. You might wonder why, under normal circumstances, a newcomer would succeed after experts *who had tried for months* had failed. _____

4-7. If you're willing to pay $60 an ounce, you can serve your guests Beluga, *Russia's finest caviar.* _____

4-8. Few people can name *both their senators*. _____

4-9. *Although sure of the outcome*, we had no idea the score would be so lopsided. _____

4-10. *Time stands still* when you smile. _____

Exercise 5:

The italicized passage in each of the following sentences is a *phrase*. The first two are prepositional; the rest may or may not be. Opposite each one, mark whether it serves as an adjective, adverb, noun, or verb:

5-1. *In 1958*, the Russians stunned the world by launching Sputnik I, the first space satellite. _____

5-2. A child *with no toys* will quickly turn its parents into raving maniacs. _____

5-3. *A remarkable machine* can read books and talk the words to the blind. _____

5-4. It uses *a synthesized voice*. _____

5-5. Some of Margaret Mead's work *has been criticized* since her death. _____

5-6. *Photographed on the streets of San Francisco*, these dresses illustrate next summer's colorful fashions. _____

5-7. The brain has been evolving psychologically *for the past 40,000 years*. _____

5-8. The penalties *for violating the antitrust law* may be going down. _____

5-9. Most experts agree that Jim Brown was a better runner *than O. J. Simpson*. _____

5-10. Is *being lucky* as important as being good? _____

Exercise 6:

The italicized passage in each of these sentences is a *clause*. Opposite each one, mark whether it's independent or dependent:

6-1. *If the White House intends to use food as an instrument of foreign policy*, Congress may get testy. _____

6-2. Einstein never said *that some dogs have more fleas than other dogs*. _____

6-3. *I know someone* who collects and reconditions old radios. _____

6-4. *Even though it's fully repaired*, the car will never be the same. _____

6-5. *In 29 days at zero gravity the legs get almost no exercise*, and they lose about a third of their strength. _____

6-6. *Although Oliver Wendell Holmes is our most famous Supreme Court justice*, he was never chief justice. _____

6-7. If your daughter has a lot of dates, *you wonder what she's doing to be so popular*. _____

6-8. *Unemployment*, although it has gone down slightly, *is still our biggest problem*. _____

6-9. I told Smedley, *who in turn told everyone*. _____

Exercise 7:

Next to each of the following sentences, mark whether the italicized passage is a phrase or clause, and whether it is nonrestrictive or restrictive:

7-1. Some 50 cats, *descendents of cats of Ernest Hemingway*, still live in his house on Key West. _____

7-2. "Amadeus," a smash Broadway play, is *about the tragic life of Mozart*. _____

7-3. Employees *who want this insurance coverage* must fill out new forms. _____

7-4. *Although one of the most winning golfers of all time*, Jack Nicklaus had trouble winning public approval. _____

7-5. Illegitimate births have reached an all-time high *this year*. _____

7-6. We can't finish the report *until Smedley submits his statistics*. _____

Exercise 8:

Opposite each sentence below, mark whether the punctuation is correct or incorrect. If it's wrong, correct it:

8-1. The netboats, with their capacity for enormous catches are depleting the stock of fish in the lake.

_____

8-2. An increase in both horsepower and torque, combined with lower gears in the differential, improves Supra's off-the-line acceleration.

_____

8-3. The tall, now-smiling redhead, needed no further urging.

_____

8-4. In the event of your death, your unpaid balance, all the way up to $4,000 will be paid.

_____

8-5. Twist-A-Light, with its 12-inch flexible shaft sheds light to the precise spot you direct it.

_____

8-6. Alvarez, our captain also pitches.

_____

Self-Study Exercises

(Answer Key: pages 44 through 46)

AGAIN, AS IN THE PREVIOUS SECTION, compare your answers with the answer key. Pat yourself on the back briefly for your correct answers, but take advantage of the ones you got wrong—**THEY ARE YOUR LEARNING OPPORTUNITIES.** For each one you missed, read the brief explanation in the answer key. If you still feel unsure, go back to the pages in the text (listed in the answer key) and reread the explanation until you feel comfortable about the answer.

REMEMBER: Proper punctuation depends on knowing everything we've discussed about phrases and clauses.

Exercise 4:

Next to each of the following sentences is marked whether the italicized passage is a phrase, clause, or appositive:

4-1. Michael Spinks, *Leon's brother*, is also a boxer.

Appositive
Page 40.

4-2. Who wouldn't be enticed by a dinner *at LeCoq au Vin*?

Phrase
Page 37.

4-3. *Only a handful* of us stayed to the end.

Phrase
Page 37.

4-4. *Because we stayed*, however, we can now operate the equipment properly.

Clause
Page 38.

4-5. *After the long and exhausting flight to Hong Kong*, we had no chance to rest before the meeting.

Phrase
Page 37.

4-6. You might wonder why, under normal circumstances, a newcomer would succeed after experts *who had tried for months* had failed.

Clause
Page 38.

4-7. If you're willing to pay $60 an ounce, you can serve your guests Beluga, *Russia's finest caviar*.

Appositive
Page 40.

4-8. Few people can name *both their senators*.

Phrase
Page 37.

4-9. *Although sure of the outcome*, we had no idea the score would be so lopsided.

Phrase
Page 37.

4-10. *Time stands still* when you smile.

Clause
Page 38.

Exercise 5:

The italicized passage in each of the following sentences is a *phrase*. The first two are prepositional; the rest may or may not be. Opposite each one is marked whether it serves as an adjective, adverb, noun, or verb:

5-1. *In 1958*, the Russians stunned the world by launching Sputnik I, the first space satellite.

Adverb-prepositional
(modifies *stunned*)
Page 37.

5-2. A child *with no toys* will quickly turn its parents into raving maniacs.

Adjective-prepositional
(modifies *child*)
Page 37.

5-3. *A remarkable machine* can read books and talk the words to the blind.

Noun (subject of independent clause)
Page 37.

5-4. It uses *a synthesized voice*.

Noun (direct object of transitive verb uses)
Page 37.

5-5. Some of Margaret Mead's work *has been criticized* since her death.

Verb (main verb of independent clause) Page 37.

5-6. *Photographed on the streets of San Francisco*, these dresses illustrate next summer's colorful fashions.

Adjective (modifies *dresses*) Page 37.

5-7. The brain has been evolving psychologically *for the past 40,000 years*.

Adverb-prepositional (modifies *has been evolving*) Page 37.

5-8. The penalties *for violating the antitrust law* may be going down.

Adjective-prepositional (modifies *penalties*) Page 37.

5-9. Most experts agree that Jim Brown was a better runner *than O. J. Simpson*.

Adverb-prepositional (modifies *better*) Page 37.

5-10. Is *being lucky* as important as being good?

Noun (subject; order is reversed for questions) Page 37.

Exercise 6:

The italicized passage in each of these sentences is a *clause*. Opposite each one is marked whether it's independent or dependent:

6-1. *If the White House intends to use food as an instrument of foreign policy*, Congress may get testy.

Dependent Page 38.

6-2. Einstein never said *that some dogs have more fleas than other dogs*.

Dependent Page 38.

6-3. *I know someone* who collects and reconditions old radios.

Independent Page 38.

6-4. *Even though it's fully repaired*, the car will never be the same.

Dependent Page 38.

6-5. *In 29 days at zero gravity the legs get almost no exercise*, and they lose about a third of their strength.

Independent Page 38.

6-6. *Although Oliver Wendell Holmes is our most famous Supreme Court justice*, he was never chief justice.

Dependent Page 38.

6-7. If your daughter has a lot of dates, *you wonder what she's doing to be so popular*.

Independent Page 38.

6-8. *Unemployment*, although it has gone down slightly, *is still our biggest problem*.

Independent Page 38.

6-9. I told Smedley, *who in turn told everyone*.

Dependent Page 38.

Exercise 7:

Next to each of the following sentences is marked whether the italicized passage is a phrase or clause, and whether it is nonrestrictive or restrictive:

7-1. Some 50 cats, *descendents of cats of Ernest Hemingway*, still live in his house on Key West.

*Phrase
Nonrestrictive*
Page 37.

7-2. "Amadeus," a smash Broadway play, is *about the tragic life of Mozart.*

*Phrase
Restrictive*
Page 37.

7-3. Employees *who want this insurance coverage* must fill out new forms.

*Clause
Restrictive*
Page 39.

7-4. *Although one of the most winning golfers of all time,* Jack Nicklaus had trouble winning public approval.

*Phrase
Nonrestrictive*
Page 37.

7-5. Illegitimate births have reached an all-time high *this year.*

*Phrase
Restrictive*
Page 37.

7-6. We can't finish the report *until Smedley submits his statistics.*

*Clause
Restrictive*
Page 39.

Exercise 8:

Opposite each sentence below is marked whether the punctuation was correct or incorrect. If it was wrong, it is corrected here:

8-1. The netboats, with their capacity for enormous catches, are depleting the stock of fish in the lake. (Corrected.)

Incorrect
Page 37.

8-2. An increase in both horsepower and torque, combined with lower gears in the differential, improves Supra's off-the-line acceleration.

Correct
Page 37.

8-3. The tall, now-smiling redhead needed no further urging. (Corrected.)

Incorrect
Page 37.

8-4. In the event of your death, your unpaid balance all the way up to $4,000 will be paid. (Corrected.) (But note: You could, if you wish, leave out the comma after the short introductory phrase [. . . death your . . .].)

Incorrect
Page 37.

8-5. Twist-A-Light, with its 12-inch flexible shaft, sheds light to the precise spot you direct it. (Corrected.)

Incorrect
Page 37.

8-6. Alvarez, our captain, also pitches. (Corrected.)

Incorrect
Page 40.

(But note: The original would be correct if you were talking to someone named Alvarez.)

AGAIN, AS IN THE PREVIOUS SECTION, compare your answers with the answer key. Pat yourself on the back briefly for your correct answers, but take advantage of the ones you got wrong—**THEY ARE YOUR LEARNING OPPORTUNITIES.** For each one you missed, read the brief explanation in the answer key. If you still feel unsure, go back to the pages in the text (listed in the answer key) and reread the explanation until you feel comfortable about it.

REMEMBER: Proper punctuation depends on knowing everything we've discussed about phrases and clauses.

The Noble English Sentence

The Noble English Sentence

It was Winston Churchill who called the simple English sentence "noble." And if sentences can be noble, the use of language to simplify ideas—to convey as much knowledge as possible to as many people as possible—is divine.

All the rules of grammar, including punctuation, serve one purpose: to help writers construct *individual sentences*, one at a time, that are clear to the reader. If you can do that, you can write anything your brain is capable of thinking.

Always remember: A sentence contains a complete idea. It is capable of standing alone and making sense, in the context of your writing, without any other words or punctuation marks. In writing, the sentence is the basic vehicle of the idea.

The mastery of basic grammar will make your writing acceptable. The mastery of syntax, which is the part of grammar that deals with the arrangement of words within sentences (discussed later in this chapter), can make it outstanding—even artistic.

There are four basic kinds of sentences: simple, compound, complex, and compound/complex.

The Simple Sentence

A simple sentence is one that contains one independent clause and no dependent clauses (see pages 38 and 39). *The waiter poured the coffee*. But don't be confused. This is also a simple sentence: *A majority of House members*, (subject) *lobbied with understandable but simplistic ferocity by the United Auto Workers, this week began* (verb) *seeking to pass a bill forcing foreign auto makers to build their cars in the United States or suffer the consequences of the application of much-tightened import quotas*. That's a terribly complicated sentence. But it's a *simple* sentence in that it contains just one independent clause; all the rest consists of phrases and other modifiers. (And, although it is grammatically correct, it is an awkward sentence for reasons we'll discuss under Syntax.)

The two most basic parts of every sentence are a subject and an action. Usually (but not always) the subject performs that action. (Sometimes the subject *receives* the action; see passive voice verbs, page 90.) The subject is always a noun, or a pronoun (standing for a noun). The action is described by a verb. The basic parts of any sentence, then, are its subject and verb. But each of those in turn can consist of several smaller parts. *Levitt and the people he represents* (subject) *demand* (verb) *a cleanup by next year* (object) *and will be satisfied only upon approval of funding for it* (phrase). That is still a simple sentence; there is still only one clause.

Because so many variations of subject and verb are possible, it's useful to think in terms of *subject* and *predicate*. The person, thing, or place performing the act is the subject. The predicate contains the verb; it tells you what the action is (or was, or will be).

Smedley, the manager of our accounts receivable department (subject), *received her Ph.D in Business Administration last week, after four years of study* (predicate). In that sentence, the simple subject is *Smedley*; and the simple verb is *received*. But everything from *received* to the end of the sentence is the predicate; it is all part of the action performed by the subject.

Let's break down predicates a little further.

The basic structure of the most common simple sentence (in English) is: *subject, transitive verb, direct object*. That structure is the backbone of the English language, and you probably learned those terms (or should have) early in your education. Transitive comes from the Latin *trans* or *across*; the *transitive* verb, then, takes the action *across* from the subject to the object.

Settembrini (subject) *raises* (transitive verb) *Siamese cats* (direct object).

Note that you can't stop at the verb when it is transitive; the verb needs to be directed somewhere. You can't say *Settembrini raises*; a listener would ask, "Yes? Go on." The sentence demands a direct object.

A *complement*, when a sentence contains one, *completes* the action of the verb; like the verb, it's part of the predicate. In the *subject-transitive verb-direct object* structure, the direct object is usually the complement; it completes the action of the transitive verb. (Smedley, the manager of our accounts receivable department, *received* [transitive verb] *her Ph.D. in Business Administration* [direct object–complement] last week, after . . . .)

But not all verbs need a complement. Some verbs are *intransitive*—that is, nothing needs to receive the action. There are two kinds of intransitive verbs. *Complete* verbs need nothing more (She *snores*; I *lied*). The verb is the whole predicate; no complement is needed. *Linking* verbs do need a complement, but that complement is not a direct object. For example, *The potato salad tasted . . .* Now, you can't stop there; a listener would ask, "Yes? Go on." We know that the potato salad did not *taste something*, so the verb *taste* is not transitive. In this case it's an intransitive *linking* verb, and our computer brain tells us intuitively that the rest of the sentence (complement) must tell us not *what* the potato salad tasted but *how* it tasted. The types of complements that do this for linking verbs are *predicate adjectives* or *predicate nominatives: The potato salad tasted terrible* (predicate adjective). But if the linking verb requires a *what*, not a *how*, the complement will be a noun called *predicate nominative: The potato salad was the main course* (noun). (See comments on predicate adjectives and predicate nominatives, page 122.)

Compound, Complex, and Compound/Complex Sentences

A compound sentence contains two or more independent clauses, and they are joined by a comma and one of the coordinate conjunctions (*and, but, or, nor, for, so, yet*). Because they are independent, each of the separate clauses is capable of standing alone as a separate sentence.

We got there late, but the program hadn't started yet.
Try using the alpha-numeric code, and be sure to fill out the evaluation form completely.

But not:

Try using the alpha-numeric code, being sure to fill out the evaluation form completely. In that one, the second part is a phrase (no subject), not a clause. Sorry, no compound sentence.

A complex sentence contains one independent clause and at least one dependent or subordinate clause.

We're going to run the entire test again when the adjustments are completed.

Note that *We're going to run the entire test again* can stand alone; *when the adjustments are completed* cannot.

Because the game is Tuesday night, we've postponed the meeting.

Because the game is Tuesday night cannot stand alone; *we've postponed the meeting* can.

A compound/complex sentence, as its name implies, combines both. It contains two or more independent clauses, making it compound, and at least one of

Hopefully— let's end this controversy

The newscaster says, "*Hopefully, the fierce fighting will end soon.*"

Language purists argue that fights can't hope anything and that people who write such structures are literary slobs. You ought to know what is involved, so you can decide for yourself.

Hopefully means: full of hope. The example above, then, describes fighting that was full of hope. How can *fighting* hope anything?

The grammatical point is this: When an adverb modifies a verb, it should fit sensibly with that verb's subject. At least, they should not make a foolish statement when matched together. Sometimes they do: *Hopefully, everyone guilty of this offense will be punished.* Do those guilty people really hope to be punished?

But some excellent writers argue that the meanings of the above examples cannot be misunderstood, and, therefore, they do not sound foolish. Furthermore, they point out, there is precedent for this usage throughout English, with such words as *Fortunately, Undoubtedly.* (These, however, may be similarly misused: *Undoubtedly, Congress will refuse to approve the Bill until some confusing points are settled.*)

A more practical question than *Who's right?* is: *Why invite controversy when it's so easy to avoid?* Ask yourself each time you're tempted to write *Hopefully:* Who hopes? Then begin, "*The government hopes . . . .*" or "*The guerillas hope . . . .*" or "*I hope . . . .*" Or, if you don't want to tell, use the passive: "*It is hoped . . . .*" (see page 90).

them has a dependent or subordinate clause, making it complex.

Dimethyl sulfoxide, when it is used with medical supervision, is effective in relieving arthritic pain, but it is a highly controversial substance.

Note that the division between the compound and complex (or in this case complex and compound) parts occurs at the conjunction *but.* In the first part, *when it is used with medical supervision* is a nonrestrictive dependent clause (and therefore surrounded by commas). The second part is a simple independent clause joined to the other by a coordinate conjunction.

More About Objects. Direct objects (of transitive verbs) aren't the only kind. You will need to know about two others if you are to choose the correct pronouns in key situations: indirect objects, and objects of prepositions.

Indirect objects. Not all sentences contain them. Think of an indirect object as a secondary object—always secondary to the direct object. In the famed Pennsylvania Dutch construction, *Throw Momma from the train a kiss,* Momma isn't being thrown; a kiss is. That kiss is the direct object (of the transitive verb *throw*); Momma is the indirect object (of the implied preposition *to*). (The subject is *you* [also implied].) The relationships would be the same, but not as funny, if the sentence were in the more natural construction: Throw Momma a kiss from the train.

The same is true of an ordinary, everyday sentence such as: *I sent Maxin the photos by express mail.* Here we have the basic subject-transitive verb-direct object structure. The subject and verb are obvious: *I sent.* But watch out, now. What's the direct object? Surely *Maxin* was not sent by express mail; *the photos* were, and they are the direct object. *Maxin* is the indirect object (again of the implied preposition *to*).

The Review Committee studied *the proposal* (direct object). But: The Review Committee gave *the proposal* (indirect object) careful study. Smedley showed *us* (indirect object) their evaluation.

Objects of Prepositions. A prepositional phrase always contains (at least) a preposition and its object. (See page 37.) That object is always a noun or pronoun; there may also be modifiers. *We got the sheet music from the heavyset librarian. From* (preposition); *librarian* (its object); *the heavyset* (adjectives modifying the noun *librarian*). *That book on your desk contains all the answers. On* (preposition); *desk* (its object).

Why should you care? Recognizing whether something (or someone) is a subject or object is important. You should practice until you can tell quickly and easily. This skill will help you select pronouns correctly and avoid some embarrassments. For example, *He and I talked to Smedley* is perfectly correct grammar, but *Smedley talked to he and I* is an unforgivable error. How do you tell which is which? One way is correct for subjects, the other for objects. (See page 77.) The same is true for *who* and *whom.* (See page 100.)

Syntax: The Art of Making Sentences Effective

This sentence is grammatically correct:

> *The network of four gas chromatographs, which will be controlled by the SR-4100 system, and which was designed and assembled at our lab under the direction of Dr. Fischer, who last year won the Granville Award for his work on radioisotopic conversion even though his analysis had been only partially tested, includes two dual-channel instruments, of which the first features an automated sample selection system coupled to an injection and backflush system, and the second utilizes standard injection techniques but features automated backflush valving and senses when the sample is in the ready condition.*

*About
sentence
fragments*

Even the strictest grammarians allow occasional sentences that are not grammatically complete. When you use them, however, two rules are important:

(1) Don't use them very often. (2) When you do, keep them short, so the reader will know the incomplete form is deliberate.

Used this way, a sentence fragment can be an effective rhetorical device. Sometimes, anyhow.

The opening sentence in the Foreword of this book is a fragment; it has no verb.

Even though it is grammatically correct in every way, that is a terrible sentence, and it demonstrates an important point: Good grammar alone does not make good writing; in fact it does not even ensure basic clarity.

The weaknesses are in *syntax*—the arrangement of the words, phrases, and clauses within a sentence.

Only a part of syntax involves grammar; the rest is a matter of common sense and understanding what goes on in your reader's brain as he or she receives those words, phrases, and clauses. Remember, everything you do as a writer should be for the benefit of that poor devil at the receiving end—your reader.

Two important things are wrong with that monstrous sentence at the bottom of page 50: It is much too long (94 words and several major ideas), and some important words are badly separated from the words they modify. These are common flaws among unskilled writers—especially those who are highly educated. (Less educated people probably could not keep the grammar straight in a sentence that long and complicated, and they probably wouldn't try.)

Now examine those *same ideas* again:

> *The network of four gas chromatographs includes two dual-channel instruments. The first features an automated sample selection system coupled to an injection and backflush system. The second utilizes standard injection techniques but features automated backflush valving and senses when the sample is in the ready condition. This network will be controlled by the SR-4100 system. It was designed and assembled at our lab under the direction of Dr. Fischer, who last year won the Granville Award for his work on radioisotopic conversion even though his analysis had been only partially tested.*

Note that the two versions contain exactly the same information. Not even the slightest detail is sacrificed in the second (simpler) one.

Keep most sentences short and simple. The most obvious difference between the two versions above is that the first was one monstrously long sentence of 94 words, and the second was five sentences totaling 91 words and averaging 18.2 words each. The first consisted of one main clause interwoven with five dependent clauses; the second contained four independent clauses (simple sentences) and one complex sentence containing an independent and two dependent clauses.

Note, too, that the simpler version ended up shorter; 94 words became 91. Brevity is not one of the most important considerations in writing, and if you need more words to be clear you should take them. But it's interesting to note that so often the clearer way is also the shorter way of saying something.

Outstanding writers almost invariably compose sentences that average between 15 and 20 words in length. Notice, however, the emphasis on the word *average*. Don't write *all* sentences within those limits, because doing so would make your style so dull it would bore readers. Mix them up. Although probably not aware of it, readers feel most comfortable with the changing pace they experience when the sentences are occasionally as short as two or three words or as long as 30 or 35. A sentence can be as short as two words (subject and verb), and there is every reason to think you should occasionally write one that short. (You will find, incidentally, that short sentences are easier to write than long ones; you become stuck less often.) At the other extreme, there is no limit to how long a sentence can be—in *theory*. In practice, however, there are two very real limits: your ability to keep the grammar correct, and your reader's ability to follow the ideas. In practice, then, sentences can be as long as 30 or 35 words; rarely should they go much longer.

Within those limits, you will find all the freedom for artistry and self-expression that any writer needs.

Short sentences give emphasis. The shorter they are, the harder they hit. They also

How long should sentences be?

There are reasons your favorite authors are your favorites. Skilled writers do many things with language to create exactly the mood they want, and one of the most effective is control of sentence length.

Brevity creates emphasis; the shorter a sentence is, the harder it hits. Short sentences also create the feeling of action, because shorter means more sentences and therefore more verbs.

Long sentences, on the other hand, are generally useful for the slower pace desirable in descriptive passages, meandering along like peaceful stretches of a river, at the relaxed speed best suited for detailed viewing of the less important information that provides the background for the action passages.

Good writing is almost always a mixture of the two.

Good writing almost always averages between 15 and 20 words per sentence. Don't write *all* sentences within those limits, however. Mix them up. Readers will feel bored if all your sentences are approximately the same length, regardless that length. The shortest sentence in this passage is 3 words, the longest is 47, and the average is 16.2 words per sentence.

For most educated adults, averaging between 15 and 20 words per sentence requires shortening (chopping) some long ones. For most children, it requires lengthening (combining) some short ones.

The flight attendant announced, *"While in the aircraft you may only smoke in your seat."*

Wow! The airline would (we hope) allow passengers to do many other things in their seats. If nothing else, they ought to be permitted to breathe.

For decades, language purists have complained that many writers position *only* **incorrectly when it's an adverb. (It can also be an adjective:** *The only person . . . .* **) They are right, but their argument is a bit weak because the error does not usually change the meaning or create awkwardness. (If it did either, the author would probably notice and correct it.)**

Remind yourself that *only,* **by definition, limits the word it modifies to** *one* **of something (one-ly). Be sure it's the right thing.** *"While in the aircraft you may only . . . ."* **Now stop there, and think. Because** *may* **is the beginning of some verb, what follows** *only* **is the rest of that verb, and that is what is limited by** *only* **(***only smoke***). The trouble is, it shouldn't; there are several other things passengers may do in their seats, besides smoke. The intended statement, of course, was:** *"While in the aircraft you may smoke only in your seat."*

Best advice: Place *only* **as close as possible to the word or phrase it limits. You will do that anyhow, if you are good at syntax (see page 50).**

create the feeling of action. This is because shorter sentences mean more sentences and therefore more verbs. Verbs are the action words, and skilled writers deliberately use short sentences to create the tense, fast-moving mood appropriate for action passages. (*That passage contained 11 words per sentence—okay for short passages but too short for sustained reading* [*for adults*]*.*)

Long sentences, on the other hand, are generally useful for the slower pace necessary in descriptive passages, which are as important for proper balance as the action. They meander along, like peaceful stretches of a river, at the relaxed speed best suited for detailed viewing, slowly, deliberately unfolding information about the people, places, and things that provide the background for the actions. Although an important part of most writing, such sentences tend to subordinate the ideas they contain and therefore are generally ineffective for presenting major ideas. (*That passage contained 29 words per sentence—much too long for sustained reading. Longest sentence: 35 words.*)

It is the combination of those two techniques that causes readers to say, "I enjoyed reading this."

Keep related words close together. Modifiers should be close to the words they modify. Pronouns should be close to the nouns they stand for (their antecedents). Especially, subjects and their verbs should be close together. *Never separate a subject from its verb by very much other information; the reader may not be able to match the two, and the result is chaos.* (In the 94-word passage on page 50, the subject of the main clause [*network*] is separated from its verb [*includes*] by three other clauses—three other subjects and verbs.) Such constructions are put on paper by klutzes and slobs, not writers.

This is not to say you shouldn't use subordinate clauses; such advice would be unthinkable. Subordinate (dependent) clauses are marvelously useful because they do exactly what their name implies: They signal that some facts in your writing are subordinate to (less important than) others. The trouble is that some unskilled writers, perhaps trying to appear literary by using long sentences, put vital information into subordinate clauses. That simply doesn't make sense. You are not being reasonable if you expect readers to feel an idea is important when you, the writer, treat it as though it were unimportant.

Putting a clause or phrase into another is called *embedding*. It is not always wrong, but it is an invitation to trouble.

The report, which was prepared by a panel of prominent educators appointed by President Reagan, shocked Americans by stating we would view it as an act of war if a foreign power had attempted to impose on America the mediocre education performance that exists today. (45 words.)

That construction invites readers to ignore the subordinate clause and the information it contains. The writer treated as incidental the idea that the report was prepared by a panel of prominent educators and that they were appointed by the President; why, then, shouldn't the reader also consider it unimporant? The two major ideas compete for the reader's attention. One dominates, and the other goes partly unnoticed; or they share equally, neither getting the full attention it deserves. Try:

The report shocked Americans by stating we would view it as an act of war if a foreign power had attempted to impose on America the mediocre educational performance that exists today. It was prepared by a panel of prominent educators appointed by President Reagan. (Still 45 words.)

or

The report was prepared by a panel of prominent educators appointed by President Reagan. It shocked Americans by stating we would view it as an act of war if a foreign power had attempted to impose on America the mediocre education performance that exists today. (Still 45 words.)

Exercise 9:

Circle the subject in each of these sentences, draw a box around the predicate, and underline the main verb:

9-1. Researchers have announced the discovery of human genes that are capable of turning ordinary cells into malignant ones.

9-2. A marsh in Wyoming, because of our work, is becoming a virtual wildlife refuge.

9-3. The Surgeon General has determined that cigarette smoking is dangerous to your health.

9-4. Illegal catches of salmon in England have become so heavy that in some areas they are double the legal catch.

9-5. According to our records this shipment, which left our plant in mid-August, has been sitting on your receiving dock for two weeks.

9-6. All of us in the department miss you and hope you will return soon, fully recovered.

9-7. Can you remove the fabric from the front panels?

9-8. Paying the whole bill at once may be a problem.

9-9. The parents of the bitten child complained that the dog should have been placed under quarantine.

9-10. On second down with inches to go for a touchdown, he threw a pass that was intercepted.

Exercise 10:

Mark whether each of these sentences is simple, compound, complex, or compound/complex:

10-1. I love you. _____

10-2. This new optical fiber, with a core only one-sixth as thick as a human hair, will improve transmission. _____

10-3. Bank failures, which averaged fewer than ten a year in the 1960's and 1970's, are now occurring at a worrysome rate. _____

10-4. Both sides have made false claims in the past, and it is difficult to know who is telling the truth. _____

10-5. The sexy actress failed her fund-raising audition with the National Committee, which plans to edit her out of its nationally televised Memorial Day Telethon.

_____

10-6. College athletes who have won national recognition are accustomed to being treated as heroes on the campus, and they often find entry into the pros to be a rude shock.

_____

10-7. Despite Libya's intervention in Chad and the public furor over the conviction of a former CIA agent for smuggling U.S. arms to Libya, agents of the Kaddafi regime continue to seek the aid of U.S. businessmen in acquiring American military equipment.

_____

10-8. I failed, but others who follow me will succeed.

_____

10-9. No one in this organization has the authority to tell you what to do, but if sensible you will listen to good advice and decide on the basis of the greatest benefit to the organization, not to you.

_____

10-10. An aspirin a day can keep heart attack away, according to a striking new report from the Veterans Administration.

_____

Exercise 11:

Underline the direct object (part of the predicate) in each of these sentences:

11-1. The success of the play surprised everyone.

11-2. Paul Bunyan had a blue ox named Babe.

11-3. Whom do you want?

11-4. You have, whether you realize or not, the power to end this crisis.

11-5. I hate the way Gregory laughs.

11-6. Ontogeny recapitulates phylogeny.

11-7. We will send you a copy of the report.

11-8. Few people have enough buoyancy to swim very long with their heads above water without becoming extremely fatigued.

11-9. Bring me the apples.

11-10. The alfalfa plant, though it grows to a height of only 2 feet, has remarkable 40-foot roots.

Exercise 12:

Identify all *objects* in these sentences. Draw a single underline for direct objects (of transitive verbs), a double underline for indirect objects, and a triple underline for objects of prepositions.

12-1. The radar penetrated the fog, and our pilot flew through it easily.

12-2. For several reasons, the Agriculture Department has reopened the hearings on food stamp eligibility.

12-3. The American Camel Racing Derby is held in Virginia City, Nevada, every year.

12-4. Don't give me trouble about this, you jerk.

12-5. Teamster members overwhelmingly rejected the appointment of Collier, even though their president had fought for his approval, and that rejection surprised me.

12-6. They are perfect.

12-7. The study mentions you in several sections, so I am sending you a copy.

12-8. I wear gloves for gardening, to protect me from bugs.

12-9. By the time they had finished the speech, it sounded like a TV commercial.

12-10. Soviet scientists use small submarines for research throughout the world.

Exercise 13:

Divide each of the sentences below into two or more shorter ones. (You may have to add or change a few words; remember, the new grammatical structures must be capable of standing alone as complete sentences.)

13-1. Because each company has its own identity and its own successful way of doing things, the idea of all of them being sort of molded into a general image after the merger is probably dangerous and unnecessary.

_____

_____

_____

13-2. Since all kinds of experts have been predicting that a water shortage in the near future will hinder further industrial growth in the Southwest, state and city planners in the Great Lakes area of the United States, where fresh water is a plentiful commodity, are hopeful that the shift in the industrial growth will reverse itself in the next 15 or 20 years.

_____

_____

_____

_____

_____

13-3. This new document, which defines the terms of your insurance coverage in plain English, now becomes part of the policy and should be kept in your files with the policy.

_____

_____

_____

13-4. I don't know how we're going to do this, but I am certain that we will do it, and it will be on time.

_____

_____

13-5. Even though most diplomats are convinced that the policy cannot succeed and that in the long run it will hurt the President, the majority of them are backing the President in his struggle with Congress.

_____

_____

_____

13-6. Roger Maris hit more home runs in one season than Babe Ruth but is not considered as great a hitter because the season was longer.

_____

_____

Exercise 9:

A circle is drawn around the subject in each of these sentences and a box around the predicate, and the main verb is underlined:

9-1. (Researchers) have announced the discovery of human genes that are capable of turning ordinary cells into malignant ones.   Page 48

9-2. A (marsh) in Wyoming, because of our work, is becoming a virtual wildlife refuge.   Page 48

9-3. The (Surgeon General) has determined that cigarette smoking is dangerous to your health.   Page 48

9-4. Illegal (catches) of salmon in England have become so heavy that in some areas they are double the legal catch.   Page 48

9-5. According to our records this (shipment) which left our plant in mid-August, has been sitting on your receiving dock for two weeks.   Page 48

9-6. (All) of us in the department miss you and hope you will return soon, fully recovered.   Page 48

9-7. Can (you) remove the fabric from the front panels?   Page 48

9-8. (Paying) the whole bill at once may be a problem.   Page 48

9-9. The (parents) of the bitten child complained that the dog should have been placed under quarantine.   Page 48

9-10. On second down with inches to go for a touchdown, (he) threw a pass that was intercepted   Page 48

Exercise 10:

Each of these sentences is marked simple, compound, complex, or compound/complex:

10-1. I love you.

Simple
Page 49

10-2. This new optical fiber, with a core only one-sixth as thick as a human hair, will improve transmission.

Simple
Page 49

10-3. Bank failures, which averaged fewer than ten a year in the 1960's and 1970's, are now occurring at a worrysome rate.

Complex
Page 49

10-4. Both sides have made false claims in the past, and it is difficult to know who is telling the truth.

Compound/Complex
Page 50

10-5. The sexy actress failed her fund-raising audition with the National Committee, which plans to edit her out of its nationally televised Memorial Day Telethon.

Complex
Page 49

10-6. College athletes who have won national recognition are accustomed to being treated as heroes on the campus, and they often find entry into the pros to be a rude shock.

Compound/Complex
Page 50

10-7. Despite Libya's intervention in Chad and the public furor over the conviction of a former CIA agent for smuggling U.S. arms to Libya, agents of the Kaddafi regime continue to seek the aid of U.S. businessmen in acquiring American military equipment.

Simple
Page 48

10-8. I failed, but others who follow me will succeed.

Compound/Complex
Page 50

10-9. No one in this organization has the authority to tell you what to do, but if sensible you will listen to good advice and decide on the basis of the greatest benefit to the organization, not to you.

Compound
Page 49

10-10. An aspirin a day can keep heart attack away, according to a striking new report from the Veterans Administration.

Simple
Page 48

Exercise 11:

The direct object (part of the predicate) is underlined in each of these sentences:

11-1. The success of the play surprised everyone. Page 49

11-2. Paul Bunyan had a blue ox named Babe. Page 49

11-3. Whom do you want? Page 49

11-4. You have, whether you realize or not, the power to end this crisis. Page 49

11-5. I hate the way Gregory laughs. Page 49

11-6. Ontogeny recapitulates phylogeny. Page 49

11-7. We will send you a copy of the report. Page 49

11-8. Few people have enough buoyancy to swim very long with their heads above water without becoming extremely fatigued. Page 49

11-9. Bring me the apples. Page 49

11-10. The alfalfa plant, though it grows to a height of only 2 feet, has remarkable 40-foot roots. Page 49

Exercise 12:

All *objects* in these sentences are identified: a single underline for direct objects (of transitive verbs), a double underline for indirect objects, and a triple underline for objects of prepositions.

12-1. The radar penetrated the fog, and our pilot flew through it easily.   Page 50

12-2. For several reasons, the Agriculture Department has reopened the hearings on food stamp eligibility.   Page 50

12-3. The American Camel Racing Derby is held in Virginia City, Nevada, every year.   Page 50

12-4. Don't give me trouble about this, you jerk.   Page 50

12-5. Teamster members overwhelmingly rejected the appointment of Collier, even though their president had fought for his approval, and that rejection surprised me.   Page 50

12-6. They are perfect.   Page 50

12-7. The study mentions you in several sections, so I am sending you a copy.   Page 50

12-8. I wear gloves for gardening, to protect me from bugs.   Page 50

12-9. By the time they had finished the speech, it sounded like a TV commercial.   Page 50

12-10. Soviet scientists use small submarines for research throughout the world.   Page 50

Exercise 13:

Each of the sentences below is divided into two or more shorter ones. (In all but one, it was necessary to add or change a few words; remember, the new grammatical structures must be capable of standing alone as complete sentences.)

13-1. Because each company has its own identity and its own successful way of doing things, the idea of all of them being sort of molded into a general image after the merger is probably dangerous and unnecessary.

Each company has its own identity and its own successful way of   Page 51
doing things. Therefore, the idea of all of them being sort of molded into a general image after the merger is probably dangerous and unnecessary.

13-2. Since all kinds of experts have been predicting that a water shortage in the near future will hinder further industrial growth in the Southwest, state and city planners in the Great Lakes area of the United States, where fresh water is a plentiful commodity, are hopeful that the shift in the industrial growth will reverse itself in the next 15 or 20 years.

All kinds of experts have been predicting that a water shortage in the near future will hinder further industrial growth in the Southwest. As a result, state and city planners in the Great Lakes area of the United States, where fresh water is a plentiful commodity, are hopeful that the shift in the industrial growth will reverse itself in the next 15 or 20 years.

Page 51

13-3. This new document, which defines the terms of your insurance coverage in plain English, now becomes part of the policy and should be kept in your files with the policy.

This new document defines the terms of your insurance coverage in plain English. It now becomes part of the policy and should be kept in your files with the policy.

Page 51

OR

This new document, which defines the terms of your insurance policy in plain English, now becomes part of the policy. It should be kept in your files with the policy.

OR

This new document defines the terms of your insurance policy in plain English. It now becomes part of the policy. It should be kept in your files with the policy.

13-4. I don't know how we're going to do this, but I am certain that we will do it, and it will be on time.

I don't know how we're going to do this. But I am certain that we will do it, and it will be on time.

Page 51

13-5. Even though most diplomats are convinced that the policy cannot succeed and that in the long run it will hurt the President, the majority of them are backing the President in his struggle with Congress.

Most diplomats are convinced that the policy cannot succeed and that in the long run it will hurt the President. Even so, the majority of them are backing the President in his struggle with Congress.

Page 51

13-6. Roger Maris hit more home runs in one season than Babe Ruth but is not considered as great a hitter because the season was longer.

Roger Maris hit more home runs in one season than Babe Ruth. But Maris is not considered as great a hitter because the season was longer.

Page 51

Punctuation

Punctuation

If grammar may be compared to a set of traffic rules, punctuation marks are like traffic signals. They guide readers; they tell readers when to go and stop, and when to turn and in what direction.

The modern tendency is to use as little punctuation as possible, and that's probably a wholesome attitude. The question is: How much is enough? We would not want a traffic light at every corner; with none at all, however, driving would be hazardous. Likewise, reading would be tedious with a comma after every phrase but chaotic with none at all.

Punctuation marks can be divided into two categories. *Bread-and-butter* punctuation marks are the ones every writer MUST use regularly: the period and the comma. You could not write much without both of them. *Elegant* punctuation marks are all the others; most non-professional writers don't use them—or not very often—but should.

To use punctuation correctly, and to understand fully the advice in this section, you will need to understand what *phrases* and *clauses* are, and the differences between them. Likewise, the meanings of the terms *restrictive, nonrestrictive, dependent, and independent.* Page numbers are referenced wherever they will be helpful.

The Bread and Butter Marks

The Period.

Just as a capital letter signals the beginning of a sentence, a period signals the end of one. No problem here. Use periods at the ends of sentences (except when you end with a question mark or exclamation point [see page 66]). The period denotes a full stop. (In fact, in England it's called 'full stop.') Because it signals the end of a sentence, you cannot use a period in the middle of a sentence for any reason (except abbreviations).

Use periods after most, but not all, abbreviations. How do you tell which? If you would normally pronounce the term in its abbreviated form, no periods are necessary. Acronyms (words made of the initials of a compound term) usually fall into this category. We usually pronounce NASA as *Nassah* or as *En-Ay-Ess-Ay*; the periods aren't necessary (though they are acceptable). But with Dr., we say *Doctor*, not *Der.* Here the period is necessary. (But not in England.)

The Comma.

If the period is a full stop, the comma ranges from a half to a quarter stop. It tells readers to pause, helping them relate the words in their minds the way the writer intended, to ensure that readers receive the idea the writer intended.

What a difference a comma makes! There's a vast difference, for example, between: *I hereby bequeath all of my worldly possessions to the first of my offspring, who lives a good life* (implied meaning: the first one is a nice kid), and: *I hereby bequeath all of my worldly possessions to the first of my offspring who lives a good life* (one of them may turn out nice, but it's too early to tell). Both of those are grammatically correct.

And there is a major difference between: *After studying the plans, I feel sure, Smedley will approve them* (Smedley will study them), and: *After studying the plans, I feel sure Smedley will approve them* (I have studied them). Again, both versions are grammatically correct. But only one is what the writer intended to say. Which one the reader receives is a matter the careful writer should not be willing to leave to chance.

The Interrobang‽

InterroWHAT? That's right, interrobang! Mirthful language scholars invented it about a decade ago and offered it jokingly, yet seriously, to the world. (The world has not responded very excitedly.) As its name implies, an interrobang is a combination question mark and exclamation point, and its backers suggest you would use it to give added emphasis to a question—as the exclamation point does to a sentence. And you construct it the same way—by adding a vertical line. Isn't that marvelous?

You type an interrobang by typing an exclamation point over a question mark (backspacing). Unfortunately, many computers and word processors don't allow you to do that; your interrobangs are limited to those with laser printers and to standard typewriters and some electronic typewriters.

The world of serious writing is not ready for interrobangs. Still, one can imagine that some day they may gain respectability. Well, why not‽

62

Use commas in these seven situations:

To separate independent clauses in a compound sentence. (See page 49.) Remember, both halves of the sentence must be grammatically capable of standing alone, and they must be connected by one of the coordinating conjunctions: and, but, or, nor, for, so, yet. *The drug is suspected of causing cancer in test animals and cancer and birth defects in humans, and for years the FDA has opposed the manufacturer's efforts to market it as a contraceptive.*

Some writers argue that this comma isn't necessary if the two clauses are short. But how short? It would be hard to draw the line, and it isn't necessary. A safer attitude: Use a comma between the independent clauses of all compound sentences, no matter how short: *I'm going now, but I'll be back soon.*

To separate a conjunctive adverb from the main clause of a sentence. (See page 97.) Introductory words such as *therefore, however, incidentally, furthermore* need a slight pause: *However, the results may turn out unfavorable to the company.* These words, incidentally, require two commas when they appear in the middle of sentences (as here). Because they are adverbs, you can place them at the beginning (like conjunctions) or immediately next to the verb: *We decided, therefore, not to press the matter. It was, nevertheless, a fine piece of work.*

To separate an introductory phrase or clause from the main clause of a sentence. With phrases (see page 37) you get some freedom of choice. For a very short phrase (such as this one) you may omit the comma. For an introductory phrase long enough (such as this one) to cause readers trouble sensing its end and the beginning of the main clause, this comma provides an important pause and should be used. When it's an introductory *clause* (such as these two), no matter how long or short it is, the comma will help your reader and should be used. (See pages 38 and 39.)

To separate nonrestrictive phrases, clauses, or appositives from the rest of the information when they appear in the middle of a sentence. (See page 38.) These commas make an important statement. They tell readers the information between them is optional (nonrestrictive); it could be removed or ignored without changing the essential meaning of the part that remains. Be sure to use a pair: *George Gershwin, one of America's most famous composers, had an equally famous brother named Ira.* But, if that parenthetical passage begins or ends the sentence containing it, of course you need only one comma rather than a pair: *One of America's greatest composers, George Gershwin died at age 39 of a brain tumor.*

To separate the items in a series. Write: *The colors are red, white, and blue.* For a brief time, the U.S. Government Printing Office Style Manual decreed that the last of these commas (before the *and*) was optional. Many writing experts objected that confusion can result from its omission, however, and the government's style experts restored it in the next edition of the Manual. Most careful writers today do use this comma. It's called the 'serial comma'.

To separate a quoted passage from the rest of a sentence. Generally, we use a comma to set off a quotation from the words used to introduce it: *Axleblad said, "I don't think this will really solve the problem."* Or: *"I don't think," Axleblad said, "this will really solve the problem."* Well, in most cases, anyhow.

In some cases you may want to use a colon to introduce a quotation with more emphasis than the comma conveys: *The president told the employees: "We have surpassed last year's sales, and each of you deserves part of the credit."* But not: *The president said: "Phone me tomorrow."* In that one the colon overstates the point; a comma is more appropriate. Use a colon also to introduce any quotation of two or more sentences.

To provide a pause in any group of words if the absence of a comma might cause readers to misread. Time after time, writing demands that you watch carefully for situations in which the reader might turn the wrong direction if you don't

About abbreviations

Generally, don't use them. This advice may surprise you, but consider that in ordinary writing abbreviations serve only one purpose: to save space. Usually, in ordinary writing, the abbreviated form of a word does not save enough space to justify the slight awkwardness it creates.

Do use such standard abbreviations as Mr., Ms. (pronounced *Mizz*), Mrs., or Dr.

Abbreviate names of states on envelopes (but not in letters or reports). Abbreviate a person's title when it precedes that person's full name, but not when it is used with just his or her last name: *Prof.* Henry Higgins, but *Professor* Higgins; *Gen.* Douglas MacArthur, but *General* MacArthur.

When are abbreviations desirable? When space is very limited. Usually, therefore, they are widely used in tables, charts, and other graphic presentations—but not in ordinary writing.

(But: See 'Acronyms,' page 76.)

provide signals: *For the opening, segments of the play were cut out*. Traditional grammar says you may omit that comma. But then readers might begin receiving: *For the opening segments of the play, ...* After going that far, however, any thinking reader would realize the rest doesn't fit, and he or she would readjust the idea and continue reading correctly; although the punctuation is awkward, no great harm is done.

But how about: *For the opening, segments of the play that contained really torrid sex scenes or that seemed draggy in final rehearsals were cut out*. Now if the comma is removed, a reader who makes the wrong turn at that point has a long way to go (to *rehearsals*) before realizing he or she misread. Readers will not—perhaps cannot—tolerate such klutz-like workmanship for long.

In such situations, knowledge of the rules cannot substitute for careful thinking. Good writers need both.

The Elegant Punctuation Marks

Periods and commas are, of course, the most widely used punctuation marks. But there are many other marvelously useful ones that most writers seldom, if ever, use. Examine the keyboard of any typewriter. Every punctuation mark there is useful, and you ought to know how to use them all.

The Semicolon.

This is a truly elegant tool, but it is badly misunderstood and underused. Perhaps the misunderstanding comes from its name. A semicolon is not a half colon; in fact, it has nothing to do with a colon, and therefore the name is misleading. It is always used as either a semiperiod or a supercomma.

Use the semicolon as a semiperiod (half stop) when you feel that a period (full stop) would create too large a break between the ideas. Typically this occurs when the ideas are intimately related: *A hen can lay eggs without a rooster; they're simply not fertile and won't hatch into chicks*. Note that in this example both the clauses are independent; each is capable of standing alone as a full sentence. You could just as easily write . . . *without a rooster. They're . . . .* Also note that there is no conjunction between the two independent clauses when the semicolon is used instead of a comma to join independent clauses.

Use a semicolon as a supercomma to separate items which themselves contain commas—you have already used the ordinary comma and now need a slightly larger pause. For example, if you were writing a series of items and each one itself contained a series: *The colors were red, white, and blue; green, white, and orange; and red, yellow, and black*.

Or, a semicolon as a supercomma would be helpful if the ideas fit best in a compound sentence, which contains two independent clauses, or in a complex one, which contains a dependent and independent clause; and one clause, or both, might require commas (as in this sentence). To mark the main separation, you now need something that outranks the ordinary comma. The semicolon used this way protects readers from a mass of confusion. It is a mark of a thoughtful and skillful writer.

Parentheses.

Parentheses flash to the reader that the information contained (whether a word, phrase or clause) is optional reading. That information must be nonrestrictive; you must be able to lift it out of the sentence and close the gap without destroying the unity or meaning of the sentence. *Most of us believe that Connors (although right now he is emphatic) will change his mind before June 30th*.

Always use parentheses in pairs. There are no exceptions. Whenever you open a passage with one, do not fail to check and double-check that its closing mate appears where it belongs. Also, remember that parentheses signal to the reader that the infor-

---

Do periods and commas go inside or outside quotation marks?

Always inside. There are no exceptions.

Other punctuation marks may go inside or outside, but determining is easy. Place them inside where they apply only to the matter being quoted: *Smedley asked, "Can science accept the theory that some dogs have more fleas than other dogs?"*

Place marks other than periods and commas outside the quotation marks when they apply to more than just the quoted part: *Did Einstein say, "Some dogs have more fleas than other dogs"? Bernstein shocked the scientific world by calmly announcing, "Some dogs have fewer fleas than other dogs"!*

Another useful tip on quotation marks: For quotations running several paragraphs, use quotation marks to *open* every paragraph but not to close every paragraph; use them to close only the last paragraph being quoted.

mation they contain is optional. Do not, therefore, use them for important information; that would be self-defeating.

Use brackets for parentheses within parentheses (again [as here], always in pairs). Most modern typewriters have them.

The Dash.

Use dashes to mark a sudden break in thought, or to give some information added emphasis. *Many states—New York was the first—have passed laws requiring that consumer contracts be written in plain English, so the ordinary consumer can understand.* Notice that the usage here is exactly the same as parenthesis—but the separated information gets far greater emphasis. Readers no longer treat it as optional reading. The information may be a phrase or a clause, but it is nonrestrictive. Also notice that when used this way in the middle of a sentence the dashes must appear in pairs, the same as parentheses. But, unlike parentheses, you don't use a closing dash at the end of a sentence.

A slightly different use of the dash is to provide dramatic separation for an idea immediately after a main clause: *We tried everything we could—but nothing worked.* In that example, the second idea is an independent clause joined to the first by a conjunction. The regular rule calls for a comma between the two clauses. But the dash gives greater emphasis—and style. It even gives you freedom to drop the conjunction, if you wish: *We tried everything we could—nothing worked.* Furthermore, the added idea need not be a clause; it can be a phrase: *Pierpont is the hardest worker in the company—on Mondays.* Again, because this is the end of a sentence, only one dash is needed (rather than a pair).

BUT CAUTION: Don't use dashes very often. Their overuse interferes with the smooth flow of ideas and will annoy your readers.

Most typewriters do not have a separate key for the dash; you create a dash by typing two consecutive hyphens.

The Colon.

Think of the colon as a trumpet blast. It announces: Stop what you're doing, and pay attention to what follows. *The items are:* . . . . And that is the major way the colon is used. It is certainly a valuable signal to give your readers.

(Many writers say: "*The items are as follows:* . . . ." That's not a serious flaw, but the words *as follows* in this case are wasted; the colon says the same thing. It would be just as clear, and a bit crisper and therefore more interesting, without those two words. [Note the use of the colon at the beginning of this paragraph.])

Use a colon also to introduce a quotation if you want the quoted passage to have greater emphasis than a comma (ordinarily used for this purpose) would give it. Also use a colon to introduce a quotation of two or more sentences.

The Apostrophe.

Use the apostrophe to form the possessive case of nouns: *The sales representative's commission*, or *everybody's business*, or *Dr. Greenhouse's monkey.*

If a singular noun ends with *s*, you DO use the apostrophe, but the *s* after it is optional: *The Atlas's pages* . . . . or *the Atlas' pages* . . . . (Note, however, that this slight awkwardness could be avoided by changing the wording slightly: *the pages of the Atlas* . . . .) For plural nouns ending with *s*, add only the apostrophe—no *s* after it. *The players' decision*, or *the babies' mothers.*

Use the apostrophe also to replace missing letters in a contraction. *It's (it is), we're (we are), aren't (are not).*

Use the apostrophe also to form the plural of a number or a letter. *In the 1970's and '80's* . . . . or *Your R's look like N's.*

Capital letter after a colon?

No, in most cases. Yes, when the passage that follows is a full sentence and is longer than just a few words.

For example. *We can't grow peppers for one reason: rabbits love the young plants.* OR. *The committee must find solutions to three problems: poor visibility, damage to equipment, and irregular transportation schedules.* BUT. *One fact about American automobiles should not go unnoticed: They are uniquely designed for transportation needs in a country larger than all of Europe.*

The Question Mark.

No problem here. Most people know how to use question marks properly; you end questions with them, as you end sentences with periods.

The trouble is, most writers don't use questions in their writing. Why not? They are as useful in writing as in speech, and there is little reason to deprive yourself of them.

The Exclamation Point.

Most writers should not need the exclamation point very often. But when you need it, how marvelously it performs! An exclamation point is a period with a bang. Not much of a bang, but enough that it signals to the reader that the writer wanted emphasis here.

Quotation Marks.

Generally speaking, use them only for quotations. Do not use them unless you are repeating the exact words of the person being quoted. Always use them in pairs. Use single quotation marks for a quotation within a quotation. (On most typewriters the apostrophe is used for this.)

We say *generally speaking* because some writers use quotation marks another way—not for quotations but to notify the reader that a word or phrase is being used in some unusual way: *The air seemed "stuffy" after the storm.* The writer seems almost to be apologizing for using the word. This usage of quotation marks is controversial, but most language authorities tolerate it. A wise attitude might be: If you have to apologize very often for using words, you're probably not using them very well.

The Hyphen.

Use hyphens to divide words that won't fit at the end of a line. Here, a bit of common sense is called for. Breaking a word this way is generally undesirable, and if you can avoid breaking one by lengthening (or shortening) a line by a few letters, you should do so. If you must divide, do so only between syllables (indicated in dictionaries by a dot between letters).

Use hyphens also to connect the words of a compound adjective if the absence of the hyphen could cause misunderstanding: *The model 4000 comes complete with four-channel indicators* (indicators with four channels). There is an important difference between that and: *The model 4000 comes complete with four channel indicators* (four indicators of channels). Compound adjectives may be more than two words: *Ready-to-wear clothing, faster-than-average production rate, seventy-six-year-old marathon runner.*

Ellipsis.

Three spaced dots (and you should instruct the typist to put spaces between them) in a quotation tell the reader you have deliberately left out some of the words: *Abraham Lincoln said, "My paramount objective . . . is to save the union, and is not either to save or destroy slavery."*

A little-known (and not very important) fact about ellipses: Three dots indicate the omission of words *in the middle* of a sentence. Four dots indicate that the omission continues *to the end* of a sentence; the fourth dot stands for the period.

Who decides what's correct?

Many publishing companies provide style guides for their writers. In the United States, however, the one most widely accepted as the final authority on language usage is the *United States Government Printing Office Style Manual.* Members of its Style Board are experts in the field of printing.

You can purchase the GPO Style Manual at Field Offices of the U.S. Department of Commerce in many major cities, or write: Superintendent of Documents, Government Printing Office, Washington, D.C. 20401.

Another authoritative and highly respected reference is *The Chicago Manual of Style*, published by the University of Chicago Press, 1130 South Langley Avenue, Chicago, IL 60637. Members of its Style Board are experts in all matters of style including grammar, punctuation, and usage.

Exercise 14:

Place an X in front of each sentence below that contains an error in punctuation. Then correct every error.

14-1. Professor Samuelson, who headed the project will answer your questions.

14-2. Plastex ordered five foot containers.

14-3. Engineers and scientists usually don't learn to write in college, they're sorry later.

14-4. A rabbits' foot may bring good luck to you; but it brought little to the rabbit.

14-5. When our family spent a summer on a farm in Kansas some 30 years before any of us dreamed how thoroughly computers would influence all of our lives I was fond of visiting the city with my father on Saturdays.

14-6. Last year, our station had the highest ratings in the city.

14-7. Will you please advise me when the order was shipped.

14-8. Bellin won several awards, but never talks about them.

14-9. We think the machine is far too limited in its' capability.

14-10. There is no record of the conversation but anyone who knows Steinem can guess what it was like.

14-11. Those of you who have not filled in the forms, should be sure to do so.

14-12. I can't cook but I certainly can eat.

14-13. The president asked Rosenberg, Mitchell and Cuneo to serve on the committee.

14-14. Our team set a record, 22 losses in a row.

14-15. Miss Thistlebottom, a fictitious English teacher, created by writing critic, Theodore Bernstein, gave everybody bad advice.

Exercise 15:

The procedure is the same as for the passages in Exercise 14. These are harder, however.

15-1. Humphrey Bogart, never said "Play it again Sam"; but he said "You played it for her, you can play it for me. If she can stand it I can. Play it." "Sam" is never mentioned.

15-2. Doolittle did not show the fury that mounted in him, but the next day he called for a large scale investigation.

15-3. The winners were Garcia, first place, Cusinsky, second place, and Blocker, third place.

15-4. When the new system goes into operation, Ms. McCarthy explained delays in paying employees' hospitalization claims—previously a major source of complaints will be eliminated.

15-5. The five inch woofers are rated for 100 watts of power, and use an ultramid plastic chassis to eliminate corrosion in door mountings.

15-6. I don't think this typewriter is our's, in fact the secretaries's supervisor insists its their's.

15-7. The report is divided into three major sections; commercial processes, catalysts and presumed mechanisms.

15-8. Government and private sector representatives must work together and respect each others' needs in this most difficult of projects to ensure it's correct and timely completion.

15-9. Tass, the Soviet news agency said that jet fighters had fired warning shots at the 747, and that the airliner was on a spying mission.

15-10. The annual membership dues, for an organization your company's size, are $825.

15-11. A Congressional committee has made a surprise statement about America's junk foods, they're nutritious.

15-12. U.S. manufacturers of children's clothing for many years hurt by overseas competitors who are subsidized by their governments with dollars obtained through American foreign aid, are pushing for tighter import restrictions.

15-13. He stated emphatically, that "he would not sing *The Star-Spangled Banner* because its range is too wide for his voice."

15-14. Washington officials fear, however that the killing may weaken the special relationship between the U.S. and its former colony—the deep, and emotional tie formed by shared battles against the Japanese during World War II.

15-15. Reagan appointed federal judges in charge of the case ruled that the Administration had violated the decree.

15-16. The last major league baseball player to make an unassisted triple play, was the Washington Senator's Ron Hanson (in Cleveland, in 1968).

15-17. Two finger typists, or drafters who want to keep their heads above water in an environment increasingly dominated by CAD and other systems directed through keyboards had better learn to type.

15-18. Drug abuse, according to a high ranking official is the companys' biggest problem.

15-19. Harold, cut out this "nonsense."

15-20. Athletes, who take steroids, are generally pleased with the results.

Exercise 14:

You should have put an X in front of every passage except number 6; each of the others contained at least one error in punctuation. The corrected versions are shown here:

14-1. Professor Samuelson, who headed the project, will answer your questions.

   Don't forget that second comma when a nonrestrictive clause (or phrase) comes in the middle of a sentence. Without it, all the parts don't match. Page 63.

14-2. Plastex ordered five-foot containers.

   Hyphenate compound adjectives. (Otherwise, Plastex ordered five containers for feet.) Page 66.

14-3. Engineers and scientists usually don't learn to write in college; they're sorry later.

   The semicolon connects two independent clauses without a conjunction. Page 64. (Or, . . . *college, and they're sorry later.* Or, . . . *college. They're sorry later.*)

14-4. A rabbit's foot may bring good luck to you, but it brought little to the rabbit.

   One foot, so one rabbit. (Another example that all the parts must match.) Page 75. Use a comma between independent clauses joined by a conjunction. Page 62.

14-5. When our family spent a summer on a farm in Kansas, some 30 years before any of us dreamed how thoroughly computers would influence all of our lives, I was fond of visiting the city with my father on Saturdays.

   This can go two ways. If you think of *some 30 years . . . our lives* as a non-restrictive appositive, it should be surrounded by commas. Page 40. But if you think of *When our family spent . . . all of our lives* as an introductory dependent clause (restrictive), the first comma is a hindrance; only the second one is demanded. Page 63. (In that case, *some 30 years . . . our lives* is not an appositive but a restrictive adverbial phrase [containing two restrictive dependent clauses]).

14-6. Last year our station had the highest ratings in the city.

   The original is not wrong, but if an introductory phrase is very short, the comma is optional. Page 63.

14-7. Will you please advise me when the order was shipped?

   That's a question; it needs a question mark. Page 66.

14-8. Bellin won several awards but never talks about them.

   The second half is not a clause (no subject); therefore, no comma between the halves. Page 63.

14-9. We think the machine is far too limited in its capability.

   The possessive of *it* is *its; it's* is the contraction of *it is.* There is no such word as *its'.* Page 86.

14-10. There is no record of the conversation, but anyone who knows Steinem can guess what it was like.

   Readers need a comma between two independent clauses joined by a conjunction. Page 62.

14-11. Those of you who have not filled in the forms should be sure to do so.

> The subject of the main clause is *Those*, and its verb is *should be*. There is no reason for a comma between them.

14-12. I can't cook, but I certainly can eat.

> Two independent clauses are joined by a conjunction (compound sentence). Even though both clauses are short, the comma helps the reader. Page 62.

14-13. The president asked Rosenberg, Mitchell, and Cuneo to serve on the committee.

> Use a comma to separate all items of a series, including the last one (before *and* or *or*). Page 63.

14-14. Our team set a record: 22 losses in a row.

> Use a colon as a special announcement that something follows. Page 65.

14-15. Miss Thistlebottom, a fictitious English teacher created by writing critic Theodore Bernstein, gave everybody bad advice.

> The main clause is *Miss Thistlebottom* (subject) *gave* (transitive verb) *everybody* (indirect object [of the implied preposition 'to']) *bad advice* (direct object). The rest is a nonrestrictive (appositive) phrase, so it must be surrounded by commas. Page 63. Within that phrase, the two smaller phrases *created by writing critic* and *Theodore Bernstein* are restrictive appositives, so no commas.

Exercise 15:

15-1. Humphrey Bogart never said, "Play it again, Sam." He said: "You played it for her; you can play it for me. If she can stand it, I can. Play it." Sam is never mentioned.

> There's no reason for a comma before *never*. Use commas to introduce most quotations (or use colons if you want greater emphasis). Page 63. Use a colon to introduce a quotation of two or more sentences. Page 65. The period after *Sam* seems a better choice than a semicolon because the pause that appears a few words later between *her* and *you* is begging for a semicolon, and two of them so near each other would be awkward. (Without that semicolon Bogie would have had to say: " . . . *for her, and you* . . . . " Page 62.) The *but* after *Sam*, though allowable, is deleted because it serves no purpose when we begin a new sentence there. The last comma (before *I can*) is used because it separates an introductory clause from its main clause. Page 63. *Sam* is not a quotation in the last sentence, so no quotation marks. Page 66.

15-2. Doolittle did not show the fury that mounted in him, but the next day he called for a large-scale investigation.

> Without the hyphen, Doolittle called for a large investigation of scales. Page 66.

15-3. The winners were Garcia, first place; Cusinsky, second place; and Blocker, third place.

> The semicolons here serve as supercommas. Page 64.

15-4. When the new system goes into operation, Ms. McCarthy explained, delays in paying employees' hospitalization claims—previously a major source of complaints—will be eliminated.

> Nonrestrictive clauses and phrases in the middle of a sentence must be separated from the rest **at both ends.** Page 63. The same is true if dashes are used instead of commas. *What a difference those two closing marks make!* Page 65.

15-5. The five-inch woofers are rated for 100 watts of power and use an ultramid plastic chassis to eliminate corrosion in door mountings.

> Five woofers are not rated. (Hyphenate compound adjectives.) Page 66. . . . *and use . . . in door mountings* is a phrase, not a clause (no subject), so no comma.

15-6. I don't think this typewriter is ours; in fact, the secretaries' supervisor insists it's theirs.

> The possessive of *our* is *ours*. (There is no such word as *our's*.) The semicolon is elegant here, but a period will do. Page 64. The comma after *in fact* is optional. Page 63. The possessive of *secretaries* is *secretaries'*. Page 115. The contraction of *it is* is *it's*. Page 86. And the possessive of *their* is *theirs*. (Like *our's, their's* is not a word.)

15-7. The report is divided into three major sections: commercial processes, catalysts, and presumed mechanisms.

> Use a colon to announce that something follows. Page 65. Use commas to separate items in a series—including the last item. Page 63.

15-8. Government and private sector representatives must work together and respect each other's needs in this most difficult of projects to ensure its correct and timely completion.

> Two wrong apostrophes here. The possessive of *other* is *other's*. (*Others'* is the plural form; it doesn't fit with *each*.) The possessive of *it* is *its*. Page 86.

15-9. Tass, the Soviet news agency, said that jet fighters had fired warning shots at the 747 and that the airliner was on a spying mission.

> Use commas at both ends of appositives in the middle of sentences. Page 40. Use a comma to join two independent clauses with a conjunction (compound sentence); no comma when one is dependent—unless it's introductory. Page 63.

15-10. The annual membership dues for an organization your company's size are $825. (Better syntax: . . . *dues are $825 for* . . .)

> The prepositional phrase within the commas is restrictive. No commas. Page 37.

15-11. A Congressional committee has made a surprise statement about America's junk foods: they're nutritious.

> Use a colon to announce that something important follows. Capitalize the first letter of the part after the colon if it's long and a complete sentence. Page 65.

15-12. U.S. manufacturers of children's clothing, for many years hurt by overseas competitors who are subsidized by their governments with dollars obtained through American foreign aid, are pushing for tighter import restrictions.

> The prepositional phrase, *for many years . . . through American foreign aid*, is nonrestrictive; therefore, it demands commas at both ends. Page 63. A comma after *competitors*? Yes, if you intend to say that *all* overseas competitors are subsidized. (The clause then becomes nonrestrictive and needs commas.) No, if you want to restrict that statement to *some* competitors (and that's more likely).

15-13. He stated emphatically that he would not sing *The Star-Spangled Banner* because its range is too wide for his voice.

> No reason for a comma before *that*. The clause inside the quotation marks is not a direct quotation; therefore, the quotation marks are wrong. Page 66. (The direct quotation would read; "*I will not sing* . . . . " In that case, leave the comma and omit *that* [and change *his* to *my*].)

15-14. Washington officials fear, however, that the killing may weaken the special relationship between the U.S. and its former colony—the deep and emotional tie formed by shared battles against the Japanese during World War II.

Use commas to separate a conjunctive adverb from a main clause. Page 63. No reason for a comma after *deep*. (Also note: The phrase, —*the deep . . . World War II.* would require a closing dash if it were in the middle of the sentence. Page 65.)

15-15. Reagan-appointed federal judges in charge of the case ruled that the Administration had violated the decree.

The hyphen tells readers that *Reagan-appointed* is a compound adjective and *judge* is the subject. (Without it, readers would presume *Reagan* to be the subject and would get half way through the sentence before realizing they were confused.) Page 66.

15-16. The last major-league baseball player to make an unassisted triple play was the Washington Senators' Ron Hanson (in Cleveland, in 1968).

Hyphenate compound adjectives. Page 66. Everything up to the comma serves as a noun phrase that is the subject of the simple sentence: its verb is *was*. No comma. *Senators* is plural; its possessive is *Senators'*. Page 65.

15-17. Two-finger typists, or drafters who want to keep their heads above water in an environment increasingly dominated by CAD and other systems directed through keyboards, had better learn to type.

Two typists of fingers? The hyphen prevents us from reading that. Page 66. The dependent clause, *or drafters . . . through keyboards*, is nonrestrictive; it needs commas at both ends. Page 63.

15-18. Drug abuse, according to a high-ranking official, is the company's biggest problem.

The prepositional phrase, *according to a high-ranking official*, is nonrestrictive; it needs commas at both ends. Page 63. Without the hyphen to signal a compound adjective, the ranking official is *high*. Page 66. And the possessive of *company* is *company's*. Page 65.

15-19. Harold, cut out this nonsense.

Nonsense is neither a quotation nor a word used in an unusual way; no quotation marks here. Page 66. (By the way, if *you* were writing that sentence you might want to end it with an exclamation point. Page 66.)

15-20. Athletes who take steroids are generally pleased with the results.

Surely not all athletes take steroids. The dependent clause is restrictive; no commas, please. Page 39.

The Common Mistakes

The Common Mistakes

Banish VERY?

Some people argue that it's a dull word, that rather than strengthening a statement it weakens it, and that, therefore, it should never be used.

True, you can usually find a more interesting way of heightening emphasis than by adding *very*. Although there is surely a difference between, let's say, a pretty baby and a very pretty one, the language gives us far more vivid adjectives: beautiful, gorgeous, darling, and many others.

Still, we shouldn't banish *very*. Somehow, a statement like, *We are very concerned that you may not receive all the benefits you should receive from our program . . . .* seems more satisfying with the word than without it. *Extremely* or *deeply* could substitute, but somehow they sound less sincere.

A wise attitude: The word *very* is dull in most cases, and its use probably suggests you weren't trying very hard to be imaginative. Still, we shouldn't strike it from our working vocabulary.

You will not, of course, make such klutz-like statements as *We ain't got none*, or *Them parts is too small*. But less glaring mistakes are common among ordinary, educated adults who must write things—even the highly educated. From a zoo curator: *Being a baboon who grew up wild in the jungle, I realized that Wiki had special nutritional needs.*

Although the *creating* aspect of writing is an art, that part of writing which deals with putting your ideas onto paper (after you have created them) is a *craft*. And, as with any other craft, there are certain principles that must be understood and mastered if you are to become truly skilled. Likewise, there are common mistakes that the truly skilled know how to avoid.

The most common problems are: dangling participles, subject-verb disagreement, noun-pronoun disagreement, false series, and the missing second comma.

This axiom will help you to avoid such errors: **IN GRAMMAR, RELATED PARTS MUST MATCH.**

IF THE PARTS DON'T MATCH, OR IF THEY MATCH IN A WAY THE WRITER DIDN'T ENVISION, THE SENTENCE CAN END UP SAYING SOMETHING THE WRITER NEVER INTENDED.

Dangling Participles

Of course the zoo curator was not *a baboon who grew up wild in the jungle*. Why did the writer make a statement he or she never intended? For the same reason a business executive wrote: *After discussing the things that could go wrong, the outdated machines worried the engineers.* Both these danglers are participles (verb forms or verb phrases).

The fault is that the modifier, in this case a participle (see page 121), is not in close contact with the part of the sentence it's supposed to modify; something else lies between them, and that something else ends up receiving a description the writer never intended. (Being a baboon . . . , *I*—. After discussing . . . , *the machines*—.) The modifier dangles, or wanders around, like a barnacle ready to latch onto the first big thing it bumps into. (Also see page 87.)

But there can be other kinds of danglers, besides participles: *Vital to the U.S. economy, the President is pressing for passage of the Bill*. Or: *As reconstructed by officials, the terrorists blew up the ship around midnight.*

Notice that the dangling trouble usually arises in introductory phrases. It can happen with clauses, but it's more likely with phrases because the phrase describes an action, or condition, *but it has no subject*; then immediately the subject of the main clauses follows, almost begging the reader to connect it to those words he or she just finished reading. (*As reconstructed by officials, the terrorists . . .*) If the phrase were a clause, it would require its own subject, and the mistake would not be possible: *Because she is a baboon . . . , I realized . . . .   After the engineers discussed . . . , the outdated machines . . . .   Because it is vital . . . , the President is pressing for passage of the Bill.   As the tragedy was reconstructed by officials, the terrorists . . . .* Now the actions and conditions match their sources as the writers intended.

Subject-Verb Disagreement

Singular subjects take singular verbs; plural subjects take plural verbs. There are no exceptions, and violators of this rule are linguistic weaklings who invite scorn—and deserve it.

No thinking person would write: *The solution are easy*. Why, then, did one write: *The solution to these problems, and to similar problems faced by millions of families in the eastern states, are easy*?

The sentence structure was an invitation to trouble.

Remember, whether it is a simple sentence or the most complicated one you can construct, every clause consists basically of a subject and a verb. Either, or both, may be embellished by several modifying words, phrases, or even other clauses. (See pages 37 through 40.) These may sometimes be placed between the subject of the main clause and its verb, *and that separation causes the trouble*. The more of these embellishments, the more words and grammatical relationships the writer must cope with—and take care that all the parts match—while progressing from the subject to the verb. The writer may forget, when the verb finally comes, *what was the subject, anyhow?* The tendency in this situation is to pick the closest noun, which may or may not be the right one. And that is why writing stylists so often advise, on syntax: Don't embed very much other information between a subject and its verb—or: **Keep related parts of a sentence close enough together that readers have no trouble matching them.** Better yet: Keep related parts of a sentence close enough together that readers cannot possibly mismatch them. If you do this, you, the writer, are not likely to mismatch them.

How do you avoid the trouble without limiting your freedom of style as a writer? Surely you need phrases and subordinate clauses—for subordinate ideas. (If every small idea were a separate sentence, major and minor ideas would be treated alike, and readers would have great difficulty telling them apart.) And surely some of those phrases and subordinate clauses will be embedded between subjects and verbs of main clauses. But the writer must take care that the subject and verb agree, no matter how much other information lies between them.

Now you can see why it's so important for writers to be able to identify subjects and verbs. You should be able to recognize them intuitively. If you can't, however, be aware: The longer the sentence, the greater care you should take to ensure that all the parts match.

The subject of that badly conceived sentence (in the second paragraph of this page) is *solution* (singular); its predicate, containing the verb, is (or should be) *is easy;* everything up to the verb *is* belongs to the subject. Perhaps the writer carelessly thought the subject was *problems* (plural). Singling out the key words carefully this way, you should have no trouble keeping the parts properly matched.

Sometimes a particular group of words may cause you fits in deciding the singular/plural question: *Either the manager or her assistants revises the data base every day*. Or should that be *revise*? Both are half right, because each agrees with only half of the subject. But both are also half wrong. Smart writers won't allow themselves to be snared in such a trap. Reword the idea: *Either the manager revises the data base every day, or her assistants do*. (The compound sentence gives us two subjects, each comfortably matched with the verb it needs.) **There is ALWAYS a way to keep the parts matching, and it should be easy.**

Noun-Pronoun Disagreement

The trouble with checking the accuracy, or clarity, of your own writing is that you, as a reader of your own writing, have an advantage no other reader can ever have. *You*

None ARE or none IS?

The logic behind correct usage is simple, and therefore it's easy to be sure.

None began its Anglo-Saxon life as a contraction of *not one*. In that usage it is strictly singular and requires the verb *is*. But through the centuries it gained broader usage, and today it often means *not any*. In that usage it took on the ability to be singular or plural—and to confound writers.

How to tell: First ask yourself whether you're using *none* to mean *not one* or *not any*. If it serves as *not one*, it's strictly singular: *Of all the mysteries about ships, none (not one) is more terrifying than the story of the Marie Celeste.* If it serves as *not any*, it may be singular or plural. Ask yourself, "None (not any) of what?" The answer will tell you whether you must be in the singular or plural: *None (not any) of this food (singular) is edible.* BUT *None (not any) of us (plural) are going to touch it.*

The principle here is: The noun (or pronoun) in a prepositional phrase governs the number of the verb.

If you're not sure, most experts advise, *none are* is usually safer than *none is.*

Acronyms: Mercy to your reader

An acronym is a word made of the initials of a group of words, usually of a name or a specialized term. Used properly, acronyms are acts of kindness to your reader; they replace difficult terms with simple ones.

Always spell out the full term the first time it appears in any piece of writing, then follow it immediately by the acronym in parentheses, almost as if saying, " . . . hereinafter referred to as . . . . ": Mothers Against Drunk Driving (MADD).

Warning: Don't overuse acronyms. If a sentence looks like a bowl of alphabet soup (*The CFPM reading in the CRT indicates a DRG and should be acted upon by the ASP.*), you are being inconsiderate, not merciful, to your reader.

(For other advice on abbreviations, see page 63.)

know what you're trying to say; *you* are not relying on those little black marks on the page to find out.

In an important sense this is a major *disadvantage* to every writer. You are the least typical reader in the world of your own writing. If something is wrong down there, you tend to see not what you wrote but what you *intended to write*. With its privileged information, your brain tends to fill any gaps. (This is the main reason the serious writer should never, never proofread his or her own work.)

Pronouns are especially dangerous in this respect.

Their trouble, of course, is that pronouns usually stand for something else nearby. (*pro-noun*, for a noun). That something else is called the 'antecedent'; and a pronoun and its antecedent must match each other.

Loose Antecedent. *This is the examiner's final recommendation, quite different from your earlier report, which badly upset our client.*

The trouble here is obvious: Did *the final recommendation* or *the earlier report* upset the client? Readers get a choice because the antecedent of the pronoun *which* is unclear. If you use grammar as a guide, opposite interpretations are possible. The rule of pronoun antecedents tells us: A pronoun *tends to* stand for the last noun the reader read before it. The questionable pronoun, of course, is *which*; and the last noun before it is *report*. Therefore, the rule of pronoun antecedents tells us, *your earlier report* upset the client.

Ah, if life were that simple! Further trouble arises because another rule of grammar is equally appropriate here. The commas around *quite different from your earlier report* tell us it's nonrestrictive; therefore, we can lift that phrase out of the main clause, and the main clause then reads: *This is the examiner's final recommendation, which badly upset our client.*

Which of those opposite meanings did the writer intend? No reader can tell, no matter how long or how carefully he or she studies the passage. Even if the reader notices the trouble, neither of the conflicting rules of grammar outranks the other.

It's wise to bear in mind, however, that readers are not likely to analyze such a mistake as carefully as we have examined it here. In fact, most readers won't even notice anything wrong in a sentence such as the one above. They are likely to read one interpretation or the other, unaware they had a choice.

The President has decided to veto the measure, and minority leaders consider that decision outrageous. Few Americans, we think, will agree with this point of view. Which point of view? It was clear to the writer, but readers can't tell.

How do you ensure that your pronouns have *obvious* antecedents? This is probably one of the most difficult problems—even for skilled writers. Even an understanding of the problem is no guarantee of accuracy. We can advise only: be careful. Be sensitive. Be kind to your pronouns, but be suspicious of them. And make sure each one has a proper mate.

Wrong Pronoun for the Antecedent. A midwestern disc jockey signs off every day by saying, "When you see someone without a smile, be sure to give *them* yours."

Pronouns must agree with their antecedents in gender (sex) and number. In the old days, before nonsexist writing became important, most of us would have said or written "be sure to give *him* yours," and few people would have cared or even noticed anything wrong.

Today, generic use of the pronoun *he* causes people who care about sexual equality to frown. But plural pronouns with singular antecedents cause people who care about correct grammar to frown.

That nondiscriminating disc jockey, trying to do the right thing, could have satisfied both sides if he had read his guidelines for nonsexist writing more carefully. (See page 108.)

It's true that English does not have neutral third-person personal pronouns in the singular. (*It* is third person but *impersonal.*) So, nonsexist guidelines advise: Switch to the plural. BUT YOU MUST DO SO FOR BOTH THE PRONOUN AND ITS ANTECEDENT! You will lose nothing at all by saying: *When you see people without a smile, be sure to give them yours.*

This is not to suggest, however, that the problem of mismatched pronouns and antecedents is unique to nonsexist writing. In *anything* you write, antecedent and pronoun—like subject and verb—must agree in number: singular-to-singular and plural-to-plural. They must also agree in sex: male-to-male, female-to-female, and neutral-to-neutral.

Then there is the problem of pronoun *case.* Which is correct: *he and I* or *him and me*? Both, depending on how they're used.

In English, the form of a pronoun depends on whether it is a subject or an object. If the pronoun is a subject, it takes the nominative case. *I like wine.* If it is an object, it takes the objective case. *But wine doesn't like me.* Two kinds of objects are most common: direct objects of transitive verbs, *We notified* (transitive verb) **him,** and objects of prepositions, *We sent the notice to* (preposition) **him.**

Which form is correct, then: *Between he and I* or *Between him and me?* The preposition *between* should make it obvious; the pronouns are objects and must be in the objective case: *The Smedleys sat between him and me.* (BUT NOTE: *He and I* [nominative case] sat between the Smedleys.)

Exception: the verb *to be.* One exception must be noted, however, to the general rule about pronoun case: If the main verb of the sentence is a form of the verb *to be* (was, is, will be, am, etc.), use nominative pronouns, not objective. *It is* I (not *me*) *who must make the decision.* In this construction, the pronoun is actually a predicate nominative, not an object. (See page 122.)

False Series

A normal series follows the pattern: one, two, and three. A false one follows the pattern: one, two, and C. You can't do that; **the parts don't match.**

The new cartridge will save time, money, and improve employee morale. Mastroianni's latest effort is well acted, well directed, and undoubtedly will do well at the box office.

Related parts MUST match! In both the examples above, the writer declares the intention to build three thoughts on a word they share in common. *The new cartridge will SAVE . . . .* That's a transitive verb, and it requires a direct object. The author started out to give us three of them, but he or she got careless. Direct objects must be nouns (or pronouns). The first two, *time* and *money,* are; then for the third item of the series we are set up for another noun but receive a verb (*improve*) instead. You can't do that to us, author. We readers want all the parts to match.

Mastroianni's latest effort IS . . . that's a linking verb, and it needs something to link to. The author gives us two predicate adjectives (*well acted* and *well directed*), then throws us off balance by slipping us a verb (*will do*). We'll have none of it, author. Get your parts to match.

Correcting such errant passages will be easy, as you sit writing, if you give the matter a little thought. Only slight rewording is needed. The first example above should be a series of VERBS: *The new cartridge will save time, save money, and improve employee morale.* Or, no series: *The new cartridge will save time and money, and it will improve employee morale*. And the second: *Mastroianni's latest effort is well acted, is well directed, and undoubtedly will do well at the box office*. Or: *Mastroianni's latest effort is well acted and well directed, and it undoubtedly will do well at the box office*.

The same mistake in a different form occurs when the writer presents a series of items vertically, but gets thoughtless.

> *These are the steps we must take before introducing the system*:
> A. *Replace all existing disks.*
> B. *Modify the terminals.*
> C. *The printer must be notified of the change.*

Nothing doing, writer!

Use parallel structures for parallel ideas. If *A* and *B* begin with verbs (or any other part of speech), so must *C*. It's easy, and it's important. Only slight rewording is needed: *Notify the printer of the change*. Then all the parts match.

The Missing Second Comma

We have already emphasized that nonrestrictive phrases and clauses are set off from the rest of the sentence by a pair of commas. Those commas signal something important to the reader as he or she receives your words and sentences and reconstructs them into ideas. *A pair* of commas. But many writers omit the second one. That form of mismatching qualifies them for klutzhood.

The principles of grammar and punctuation involved here are discussed in detail in other sections of this book. (See pages 37, 39, and 63.)

The only parts of the body capable of feeling heat, the doctor explained are the skin and the inside of the mouth. You should have no trouble noticing the comma is missing after *explained*: . . . *heat, the doctor explained, are* . . . .

We will, if necessary instruct the airline to return the shipment to us. That must be: *We will, if necessary, instruct* . . . .

Those commas tell the reader that the information between them is optional—not necessary for the essential meaning of the rest of the sentence. It should be possible to lift out the information between the commas and close the gap *without changing the meaning of the parts that remain*. And the reader must be able to tell quickly and easily where the non-essential information begins *and ends*. Hence, the two commas. **Those parts then match.**

Different FROM or different THAN?

Different from is always correct.

The logic: *Than* expresses degrees of comparison—larger than, faster than, more expensive than. But *different* does not allow degrees of comparison; either something is different or it isn't. (Unless you're saying something is more different than something else. Even then, *more* is the comparative adjective, not *different*.)

Some linguists argue that *different than* is occasionally more elegant: *Linebackers require different skills than defensive backs*. Granted, that's smoother and less wordy than: *Linebackers require skills different from those required by defensive backs*. But it's also grammatically wrong, though ever so slightly, and when we use *different than* we should do so with the attitude that it is incorrect but may be acceptable. You can't escape that a thing is different *from* something, not different *than* something.

But in England: different *to*.

78

Exercise 16:

Correct each of the following common errors, keeping the wording as close as possible to the original:

16-1. A variety of incinerator designs are available.

_____

16-2. Left to themselves to write, letters by most business executives contain errors in grammar or punctuation.

_____

_____

16-3. Spreading dormant oil, which you will find is easy to do but which requires warm weather in early spring will give your fruit trees more protection against bugs than any other single spray.

_____

_____

_____

16-4. Barbara Reese Taylor was the first to endorse the new method publicly. Once she tried it, Marie Ogilvie said, "Women will never go back to the old way."

_____

_____

16-5. The protesters were scruffy looking, loud, disciplined, and acted as though they might cause trouble when police began to arrive.

_____

_____

16-6. There exists several categories of membership for military organizations.

_____

_____

16-7. You can't make automatic elevators leave before they're ready; they have a mind all their own.

_____

_____

Self-Study Exercises

(Answer Key: pages 81 and 82)

16-8. Camino Real Motor Homes, the area's largest RV dealer announces its entire selection of recreational vehicles are on sale.

_____

_____

16-9. Sensing public approval of his bold action in the crisis, the situation tempted MacArthur to challenge Truman's authority, strengthen his own popularity, and he even began thinking seriously of the White House.

_____

_____

_____

16-10. We've known each other, I'm afraid more years than either you or myself will admit.

_____

_____

16-11. No matter how many times I correct him, Benjamin continues making those kind of errors.

_____

_____

16-12. After eating lunch the plane, which was delayed in Atlanta took off for Pittsburgh.

_____

_____

16-13. A variety of degree programs are offered to provide the education you'll need for career advancement.

_____

_____

16-14. Applicants must have experience in data processing, technical writing, and be under 40 years of age.

_____

_____

16-15. Being unable to concentrate uninterrupted in my office, this book was written at Key West.

_____

_____

Exercise 16:

The original (incorrect) versions are repeated before the corrected versions are given:

16-1. A variety of incinerator designs are available.

A variety . . . is available. Singular subject requires singular verb. Page 75.

16-2. Left to themselves to write, letters by most business executives contain errors in grammar or punctuation.

Left to themselves to write, most business executives write letters that contain . . . . Dangling participle. The letters aren't left to themselves to write; the executives are. Page 74.

16-3. Spreading dormant oil, which you will find is easy to do but which requires warm weather in early spring will give your fruit trees more protection against bugs than any other single spray.

. . . in early spring, will give . . . . Without the second comma, readers can't tell where the incidental material (nonrestictive clause) ends and the primary material (main clause) resumes. Page 78.

16-4. Barbara Reese Taylor was the first to endorse the new method publicly. Once she tried it, Marie Ogilvie said, "Women will never go back to the old way."

Once WHO tried it? You can't tell, no matter how long or hard you work at it, because the sentence doesn't make clear the antecedent of the prounoun she. (*Once Taylor tried it, Marie Ogilvie said . . . .* Or: *Once Marie Ogilvie tried it, she said . . . .*) Page 76.

16-5. The protesters were scruffy looking, loud, disciplined, and acted as though they might cause trouble when police began to arrive.

The protesters were scruffy looking, loud, and disciplined. They acted . . . . False series. Page 77.

16-6. There exists several categories of membership for military organizations.

There exist several categories . . . . Plural subject (categories) demands plural verb. Page 75.

16-7. You can't make automatic elevators leave before they're ready; they have a mind all their own.

. . . ready; they have minds . . . . The error here is not really in grammar but in logic (or common sense). Subject and verb agree, and so do noun and pronoun. Subject (they) and *direct object* (mind) disagree. It's not likely the author envisioned one cosmic super-mind controlling all elevators. If he or she did, however, the original version is correct.

16-8. Camino Real Motor Homes, the area's largest RV dealer announces its entire selection of recreational vehicles are on sale.

Two errors: *. . . dealer, announces . . . .* The closing comma for a nonrestrictive phrase. Page 78. And: *. . . selection of vehicles is on sale.* Singular subject (selection) demands a singular verb. Page 75.

16-9. Sensing public approval of his bold action in the crisis, the situation tempted MacArthur to challenge Truman's authority, strengthen his own popularity, and he even began thinking seriously of the White House.

Two errors: *. . . in the crisis, MacArthur was tempted by the situation . . . .* Dangling participle. The situation didn't sense public approval; MacArthur did. Page 74. And: *. . . to challenge Truman's authority, strengthen his own popularity, and even begin thinking . . . .* False series. Page 77.

16-10. We've known each other, I'm afraid more years than either you or myself will admit.

Two errors: *. . . each other, I'm afraid, more years . . . .* Again, the second comma must tell where the incidental material (in this case a very short nonrestrictive clause) ends and the main information resumes. Page 78. And *. . . than you or I will admit.* The pronoun here serves as a subject (of a dependent clause). Page 77. If it were an object, however, *myself* would still be wrong; *me* would be correct.

16-11. No matter how many times I correct him, Benjamin continues making those kind of errors.

. . . those kinds of errors. OR: *. . . that kind of error.* (OR: *. . . errors of that kind.*) Whichever wording you choose, the noun (*kind* or *kinds*) and pronoun (*that* or *those*) must be both singular or both plural. ALL THE PARTS MUST MATCH. Page 75.

16-12. After eating lunch the plane, which was delayed in Atlanta took off for Pittsburgh.

Two errors: *After we ate lunch, the plane . . . .* Dangling participle. The plane did not eat lunch. Page 74. And: *. . . the plane, which was delayed in Atlanta, took off . . . .* Nonrestrictive clauses must have commas at both ends, so readers can separate the optional information from the main clause. Page 78.

16-13. A variety of degree programs are offered to provide the education you'll need for career advancement.

A variety of degree programs is offered . . . . Subject and verb MUST agree! Few things in grammar are more basic. In this case the subject is *variety,* (singular). The writer was probably fooled into matching the verb with the noun closest to it: *programs* (plural). Page 75. Danger of this kind of mismatch is only one of the reasons for the general advice on sentence structure: *Never separate the subject from its verb by very much other information.* Page 52.

16-14. Applicants must have experience in data processing, technical writing, and be under 40 years of age.

Applicants must have experience in data processing and technical writing. They must be . . . . False series. Being under 40 isn't one of the things applicants must have experience in. Page 77.

16-15. Being unable to concentrate uninterrupted in my office, this book was written at Key West.

Because I was unable . . . . OR: *. . . in my office, I wrote . . . .* Dangling participle. It's not the book that was unable to concentrate. Page 74.

Commonly
Misused
Words

Commonly Misused Words

Jargon: good or bad?

Jargon is the specialized language of a particular profession. It is a kind of shorthand, sometimes expressing complex ideas in a few words. In that sense it may sometimes be useful. But it has a major disadvantage: Only people in that profession can understand it.

Further trouble comes from the fact that it is also a status symbol; for this reason, writers who wish to impress with their vocabulary often seek opportunities to use jargon—in fact may invent specialized terms when none are necessary. Thus *habits* become *behavioral patterns*. Note that 'behavioral patterns' is not shorthand but triple longhand. The writing, therefore, suffers the disadvantage of jargon without gaining the advantage.

A good rule: If an idea can be expressed in ordinary English using the same or almost the same number of words, you cannot justify specialized jargon.

Remember, too: Even when your jargon is legitimate shop talk (shorthand), you should use it only in the shop. If you care to communicate, it doesn't make sense to broadcast on a wavelength the person at the other end cannot receive.

Affect/Effect. Remember them this way: Anything that *affects (verb)* something has an *effect (noun)* on it. Think of *affect* as a verb meaning: to cause change. In its most common usage, *effect* is a noun describing that change. BUT: Less common, *effect* can also be a verb meaning: to bring about, to accomplish.

Allude/Refer. A bit tricky. *Refer* means: make direct reference. *Allude* means: make indirect reference, or hint.

Among/Between. Use *between* for two people (or things) and *among* for three or more.

Anxious/Eager. *Anxious* means: nervous (feeling anxiety), and *eager* means: looking forward to.

As/Like. Winston tastes good, *as* a cigarette should. Here's why: *Like* is correct when what follows is a word or phrase; Muhammed Ali's slogan " . . . *float like a butterfly, sting like a bee* . . . . " was, therefore, perfectly correct usage. When the passage that follows is a clause (having subject and verb), *as* should be used: " . . . *as a cigarette (subject) should (verb).*"

Assume/Presume. The difference is slight. To *assume* something is to take it for granted without evidence; to *presume* something is to suppose it is true for a specific reason. A *presumption*, therefore, is usually stronger and likely to be more reliable than an *assumption*.

Assure/Ensure/Insure. These are quite different, and their correct usage should be easy. *Assure* means: make confident. (I *assure* you . . . .) *Ensure* means: make certain something will happen. (Winning this game will *ensure* we make the playoffs.) *Insure* means: to buy insurance.

Because/Since. Use *because* to denote the reason for something. (We can't finish *because* the computer is down.) Use *since* only for relations in time. (It has been down *since* early this morning.)

Between/Among. See *Among/Between*.

Can/May. Use *can* to express ability. (We *can* be there in an hour.) Use *may* to express permission. (You *may* keep that.)

Compliment/Flatter. The difference is important; they're not at all interchangeable. To *compliment* is to praise. To *flatter* is to praise insincerely, and, therefore (indirectly), to insult.

Comprise/Consist of. Almost everyone misuses these. The whole *comprises* the parts, not the other way around. Therefore: *The United States comprises 50 states.* It is not *comprised of* 50 states (the phrase *comprised of* cannot in any circumstances be correct); nor do 50 states *comprise* the United States.

Continual/Continuous. *Continual* means: frequently repeated. (There could be interruptions). *Continuous* means: uninterrupted.

Convince/Persuade. *Convince* should be thought of as the extreme form of *persuade*; when you *convince* someone you *persuade* him or her beyond any doubt.

Data are/Data is. Either form is correct. If English followed Latin rules, we would need *data are/datum is*. But English is not a Romance language and does not follow

Latin rules—even with borrowed words. (See: "About English," page 14.) If *data is* sounds better to you, use it.

Delusion/Illusion. A *delusion* is a mistaken idea, a false belief. An *illusion* is an unreal image, such as a mirage. When a magician seems to saw an assistant in half, that's an *illusion*; if you believe it really happened, that's a *delusion*. Also see: *Allusion (allude)*.

Different from/Different than. See page 78.

Disinterested/Uninterested. *Disinterested* means: impartial. *Uninterested* means: not interested. You can be *disinterested* yet very *interested*.

Eager/Anxious. See: *Anxious/Eager*.

Effect/Affect. See: *Affect/Effect*.

e.g./i.e. *e.g.* stands for *exempli gratia*; it means: for example. *i.e.* stands for *id est*; it means: that is, (or) that is to say.

Emigrate/Immigrate. They're opposites. You *emigrate* from a country; you *immigrate* to a country.

Eminent/Imminent. They're unrelated; they only sound alike. *Eminent* means: distinguished or outstanding. *Imminent* means: about to happen.

Ensure. See: *Assure/Ensure/Insure*.

Eternity/Infinity. *Eternity* means: unending time, forever. *Infinity* means: unending distance or quantity (but not time).

Evoke/Invoke. *Evoke* means: bring out. (The statement *evoked* anger from the audience.) *Invoke* means: call upon, usually referring to religious authority (as, *invoking* God's mercy); or, legal authority (as, *invoking* the Fifth Amendment).

Farther/Further. Use *farther* for physical distance and *further* for everything else. *Cleveland is farther from New York than from Washington, D.C. Any further discussion of this is pointless.*

Fewer/Less. Use *fewer* for quantities you can count. (*Fewer* chairs, *fewer* people.) Use *less* for quantities that must be measured rather than counted. (Pour *less* vermouth to make martinis dry.)

Figuratively/Literally. *Literally* means: following the exact meanings of the words. *Figuratively* means: *not* following their exact meaning (hence, a *figure* of speech). A statement like, "The boss will *literally* hit the ceiling . . . ," then, probably says the opposite of what its author intended—unless the author envisions the boss climbing a ladder.

Flatter/Compliment. See: *Compliment/Flatter*.

Flaunt/Flout. *Flaunt* means: display boastfully, show off. *Flout* means: ignore, or show disrespect for. You *flaunt* your jewelry; you *flout* the law.

Fortunately/Fortuitously. They're not interchangeable. *Fortunately* means: luckily. *Fortuitously* means: by chance; it may be fortunate or unfortunate.

Fulsome/Full and wholesome. Careful! Well-intentioned people often use these interchangeably, and doing so can cause you trouble. *Fulsome* sounds like a combination of *full and wholesome*, but it is not. In fact, it means quite the opposite: *offensive, especially through exaggeration or insincerity*. Be aware, then, that *fulsome praise* is hardly a compliment.

Are double negatives positive?

Only klutzes would say, *We don't have no record of your order.* Purists contend that two negatives cancel each other, and that the statement therefore means: *It's not true that we don't have a record of your order (therefore, we do have a record).* But that's not likely to be the intended meaning.

Poor grammar is not the only reason double negatives are controversial, however.

A White House aide writes, in perfect grammar, "It's not unlikely that the President will veto the Bill if it passes Congress." Well, if it's not *un*likely, is it likely? In language, two negatives don't necessarily cancel each other, exactly. Did the writer intend something closer to likely, or unlikely? Only he or she knows.

But wait: *Not infrequently, Bruce has been unwilling to take university regulations seriously.* Not infrequently unwilling? Careful, now. Do the first two of a triple negative cancel each other, leaving an untouched single negative? That seems to be the case, but we've already said that math doesn't apply perfectly to language. The question is rhetorical, however, because few readers take the trouble to search for the intended meaning of such mind benders.

Then, occasionally, there are mind *paralyzers: It has not been unusual for Smedley to show signs that charges she is unsympathetic to labor's views are not without foundation.* Let's see, now . . .

Good/Well. See page 27.

Gourmet/Gourmand. See page 91.

Hanged/Hung. *Hung* is the past tense and past participle of hang: *We hung the parts on the rack.* Use *hanged* only for criminal executions.

Healthful/Healthy. *Healthy* describes your physical condition. *Healthful* refers to the foods, climate, or activities that contribute to it. Florida, therefore, has a *healthful* (not a *healthy*) climate; it makes *you* healthy.

i.e./e.g. See: *e.g./i.e.*

Illusion/Delusion. See: *Delusion/Illusion.*

Immigrate/Emigrate. See: *Emigrate/Immigrate.*

Imminent/Eminent. See: *Eminent/Imminent.*

Imply/Infer. These are widely misused. When a speaker *implies* something, the listener *infers* it. It's the difference between sending and receiving the idea. *Imply* means: hint or suggest. *Infer* means: to believe something as a result of that hint or suggestion.

Incredible/Incredulous. The difference is easy. *Incredible* means: unbelievable. *Incredulous* means: not believing. If a statement is *incredible*, you are *incredulous*.

Infinity/Eternity. See: *Eternity/Infinity.*

Instinct/Intuition. Your *instincts* do NOT tell you when to buy and sell stocks; your *intuition* does. *Instincts* are tendencies or aptitudes born in an individual—programmed into that individual's genes, the result of the evolution of that individual's species and his or her genetic makeup. *Instinct* makes birds fly south in winter, causes spiders to spin webs, and gives people basic traits. *Intuition*, though also subconscious, comes from knowledge learned through personal experience. When you somehow know something is right but can't tell why, you're probably guided by wisdom gained through experience. That's *intuition*, not *instinct*.

Insure. See: *Assure/Ensure/Insure.*

Invoke/Evoke. See: *Evoke/Invoke.*

Irregardless/Regardless. This is easy. There is no such word as *irregardless*, and to use it is to appear a klutz. The correct word is *regardless*.

Its/It's/Its'. *Its* is the possessive of the pronoun *it*: *The kitten likes to roll on its back and play with its tail.* (You add *'s* to nouns to form the possessive [*the kitten's tail*], but never to pronouns.) *It's* is the contraction of *it is*: *It's time to go home.* There is no such word as *its'*. Banish *its'* from your vocabulary.

Last/Latter. Use *latter* for two things (or people) and *last* for three or more.

Lay/Lie. Remember them this way. *Lay* means: to PLACE something (or someone) in a horizontal position. *Lie* means: to BE in a horizontal position. *Lay your head on my shoulder. Let it lie there.* Putting it gramatically, *lay* is a transitive verb and requires a direct object (head). *Lie* is intransitive (complete) and never takes an object. The past tense of *lay* is *laid*. (I *laid* the report on your desk yesterday.) The past tense of *lie* is *lay*. (It *lay* there all day.)

Lend/Loan. These are not interchangeable, and correct usage should be easy.

Lend is a verb. (Please *lend* me ten dollars.) *Loan* is a noun. (This ten dollars is a gift, not a *loan*.) Confusion arises, however, because the past tense of the verb *lend* can be either *lent* or *loaned*.

Less/Fewer. See: *Fewer/Less*.

Libel/Slander. *Libel* is a damaging public statement made in print. *Slander* is the same damaging statement made orally.

Like/As. See: *As/Like*.

Literally/Figuratively. See: *Figuratively/Literally*.

Majority/Plurality. *Majority* means: more than 50 percent. *Plurality* means: the largest group, regardless of percentage (it can be less than 50 percent). *Majority is, or majority are*? If you use the word *majority* alone, it's singular. (The majority *is* in favor . . . .) If you refer to the majority *of something*, it's plural. (The majority of the members *are* in favor . . . .)

Marketing/Merchandising. In the business world these are related but different. *Marketing* means: all aspects of selling including hiring and managing sales personnel, planning sales campaigns, setting up stores or independent distribution outlets, advertising, and other related functions. *Merchandising* refers to sales promotion and advertising. *Merchandising*, then, is one of the functions of *marketing*.

May/Can. See: *Can/May*.

Militate/Mitigate. These only sound alike; they are totally different—in fact, almost opposites. *Militate* means: fight (from *military*), or argue. *Mitigate* means: soften, moderate. (The lawyers asked the judge to *mitigate* the sentence because the defendant was an orphan; the brutality of the crime, however, *militated* against this.)

Nauseated/Nauseous. These are not interchangeable. *Nauseous* means: nauseat*ing*; when you are *nauseous*, others become *nauseated*. (The difference is much like the difference between *poisoned* and *poisonous*.) Generally, then, people who say they feel *nauseous* mean *nauseated*.

None are/None is. See page 75.

Notable/Notorious. Both describe people of note, but *notable* is a compliment and *notorious* is slur. A *notable* scholar, (but) a *notorious* liar.

Oral/Verbal. There's much confusion here. *Oral* means: spoken (as opposed to written). *Verbal* means: having to do with words, whether spoken or written. (*Aural*, by the way, means: having to do with *hearing*.)

Parameters/Perimeters. Almost no one uses *parameters* correctly. *Parameters* are mathematical variables that stay constant in a particular situation. Even scientists and engineers have trouble with this word, and anyone else trying to use it is probably misusing it. Most common misuse: as a synonym for *limits*. (*The solution to the food crisis lies somewhere between the parameters of moral responsibility and political need*.) How did the writer get to that? Perhaps the thinking goes something like this: Limits are *boundaries*, which are *perimeters*, which sound like *parameters*.

Persecute/Prosecute. *Persecute* means: harrass, or treat unfairly. *Prosecute* means: take legal action through a court.

Perspective/Prospective. *Perspective* means: point of view. *Prospective* means: probable, or expected (from *prospect*). (The *prospective* Cy Young Award winner struck out nine . . . .)

Should participles dangle?

When a word or phrase does not properly modify the part of the sentence the writer intended that it should, it is said to 'dangle.'

Most common: Dangling Participle: *After eating dinner, the plane took off for Pittsburgh.* (Strange plane!) *Orphaned at the age of six, the Committee recognized that the child had outstanding skills in spite of his emotional problems.* (A whole Committee of orphans? Well, maybe, but not likely.)

Dangling Pronoun is probably the next most common. This occurs when the antecedent, the noun the pronoun stands for, is not clear: *You hold the hammer while I hold the nail, and when I nod my head you hit it.*

Writers should take great care to avoid such mis-modifiers. Danglers are hard to avoid because the writer knows what the relationship *should be;* therefore he or she may not notice if the words don't build precisely that relationship. The dangling pronoun is one of the hardest errors to avoid—even for skilled professional writers. See page 74.

Persuade/Convince. See: *Convince/Persuade.*

Plurality/Majority. See: *Majority/Plurality.*

Precede/Proceed. *Precede* means: go before. (Six aides *preceded* the candidate, checking that everything was in order.) *Proceed* means: advance to. (When you have finished, *proceed* to the next step.)

Presume/Assume. See: *Assume/Presume.*

Principal/Principle. *Principal* means: main (Overeating is the *principal* cause of obesity . . . .), or main person (as the *principal* of the school). *Principle* means: fundamental idea ("Put It in Writing" presents six *principles* of clarity.)

Proved/Proven. These are interchangeable (as participles), but *proven* is considered old fashioned and therefore less desirable.

Raise/Rise. A bit tricky. *Raise* is a transitive verb; you must *raise* something (its direct object). *Rise* is an intransitive (complete) verb and doesn't take an object; things (or people) *rise* by themselves. (*Raise* the fallen tree. The impurities *rise* to the top.)

Refer/Allude. See: *Allude/Refer.*

Regardless/Irregardless. See: *Irregardless/Regardless.*

Sensual/Sensuous. *Sensuous* means: pertaining to the senses, usually related to the appreciation of beauty. *Sensual* means: pertaining to physical appetites, usually related to sex.

Since/Because. See: *Because/Since.*

Slander/Libel. See: *Libel/Slander.*

Stationary/Stationery. *Stationary* means: not moving. *Stationery* means: writing paper.

That/Which. See page 92.

Their/There/They're. *Their* is the possessive of the pronoun *they. There* is an adverb referring to place (We went *there*), or expletive (*There* is no time . . .) *They're* is the contraction of *they are.*

Uninterested/Disinterested. See: *Disinterested/Uninterested.*

Unique/Unusual. These should be easy. Something is *unique* only when it's so *unusual* that it is the only one of its kind. It is, or it isn't. Nothing can be "somewhat unique," and "totally unique" is redundant.

Verbal/Oral. See: *Oral/Verbal.*

Well/Good. See page 27.

Whether/Whether or not. This isn't a serious problem, but generally the *or not* is wasted. The sentence, *We haven't decided whether to go* . . . states its idea fully. If you feel, however, that *or not* adds emphasis in a particular situation, by all means use it.

Who/Whom. See page 100.

What's a gerund?

Well, all right. It's a verb used as a noun, always ending with *-ing*. (We all attended the *hearing*.) However, not all verbs ending with *-ing* are used as nouns; most of them are just regular verbs. (We are *hearing* strange noises.)

Prefer Active Voice Verbs; Avoid Passives

Prefer Active Voice Verbs; Avoid Passives

Expletive deleted?

Some self-appointed guardians of grammar argue that it is improper to use *it* as a general term. (In the last sentence, they would say: " . . . using *it* as a general term is improper.") In so arguing, they are revealing a lack of understanding that disqualifies them as true guardians.

The term for such construction is 'expletive,'* and it applies to *there are* as well as *it is*. It is a useful construction, and there are examples of its use throughout literature. Daily, articulate men and women make such statements as, *It's raining*, or *What time is it?*

Guardians ask: "What is the antecedent of the pronoun *it*?" Pragmatists (and most grammatical purists) respond: "Direct your vigil toward more useful challenges, guardians."

In defense of the guardians, very frequent use of expletive construction creates dull prose. Take particular care to avoid sentence after sentence (or paragraph after paragraph) beginning with *It is* . . . or *There are* . . .

*Swear words are also called 'expletives'; don't confuse the two.

Almost every book or course on writing encourages the use of active voice verbs and discourages the use of passives. You should know what these terms mean, the strengths and weaknesses of each form, and when each is desirable. Yes, the passive voice is sometimes desirable.

When you were learning the basics of sentence structure in the 8th or 9th grade, your English teacher probably taught you some sentence like: *The child bounced the ball*. And you learned those basic terms: Subject, transitive verb, and direct object. (Child–bounced–ball.)

That sentence structure is the backbone of the English language. (See Page 48.) It is in the ACTIVE voice. The same thing in the passive voice would be: *The ball was bounced by the child*.

The danger. Let's make that a bit more grown up. In your writing you might say: *The auditor approved the proposal*. That is the same structure as *The child bounced the ball*—Subject, transitive verb, direct object. (Auditor–approved–proposal.)

In the passive voice, that would be: *The proposal was approved by the auditor*. Notice in the passive voice the subject is *proposal*. The verb is still *approved*, but it has picked up the auxiliary *was*. And the object now is *auditor*. **Subject and object have traded places.**

In the active voice, which is the more natural way of saying things, the subject performs the action and the object receives it. In the passive, the subject *receives* the action of the verb instead of performing it. The passive voice does not need an object. In fact, the object hangs there somewhat awkwardly. Notice that it is no longer the direct object of a transitive verb; rather, it has become the indirect object of the preposition *by*.

But the entire prepositional phrase is an unnecessary part of the grammar. Because it hangs there awkwardly, you are tempted to drop it out. When you do, the sentence reads, *The proposal was approved*. **The writing now does not tell by whom, and that is usually an important part of the information.** You see how important it is in these two samples:

> *It has been suggested that an Assignment Review Board be appointed to prevent these troubles. It should be given authority to approve job descriptions and training programs.*

That doesn't tell **by whom.** Compare it with the same statement in the active voice. The reader has no way of knowing it means:

> *The president has suggested that the union appoint an Assignment Review Board to prevent these troubles. The company should give it authority to approve job descriptions and training programs.*

Some of the information is missing in statements written in the passive voice, and the writer is usually not aware he or she has left it out.

Mary is loved. **By whom?** John? Irving? Her mother? All the boys at the singles bar? The difference is important. Yet each of those statements is the same, and unrevealing, in the passive voice.

It has been recommended that the Denver branch be closed and consolidated with our St. Louis operation. **By whom?** The manager of the Denver branch? The St. Louis operation? The president of the company? The writer knows, but he or she isn't telling. In fact, the writer may not even be aware that he or she is withholding important information.

It is believed that this procedure is unsafe. **By whom?** A special investigating committee believes? I believe?

At no time is a passive as risky as when you are writing procedures, or other written instructions. Do not write, *The statement must be updated every three months . . . .* The work might not get done. You are saying something must be done but not who must do it. The reader may not realize he or she is supposed to do it. Rather, write: *You must update the statement every three months . . .* (or whoever else). Notice the difference? The active voice is clearer and more emphatic, and, therefore, the instructions are more likely to be followed.

The passive is not always wrong. Sometimes *by whom* is obvious or not important. In a research report, for example, a scientist is usually describing his or her own work. *By whom* is obvious. And if the writer were to report that work in the active voice, the subject would repeatedly be *I*. That would be inappropriate; the passive would probably be better.

Also, in some cases you might want the emphasis on the action, not its source; in that case a passive voice construction might be desirable: *The school's fire alarm system was last inspected two years ago.* In fact, in that sentence the source of the action, which must be the subject in an active voice sentence, might be a distraction: *Springfield-Bates Company last inspected the school's fire alarm system two years ago.* (But that's not quite the same statement. An alert reader might wonder: Has anyone inspected more recently?) In this case the passive (first) version is desirable; it helped the writer to avoid distracting readers, by leaving out the distracting information (the name of the company). It placed the emphasis where the writer wanted it, on the school's fire alarm system, by making that the subject of the sentence. On the other hand, if the writer had wanted the emphasis on Springfield-Bates Company, the active (second) version would be the better of the two.

It's possible, incidentally, to use passive voice verbs without omitting the sources of the actions they describe. Simply leave in the prepositional phrase beginning with *by*. Remember, the object of that preposition would be the *subject* of the sentence in the active voice. Just by making sure it stays in the sentence, you can have passive voice verbs without leaving out **by whom:** *The school's fire alarm system was last inspected two years ago, by Springfield-Bates Company.*

Even though passive voice verbs are sometimes desirable, however, smart writers are aware that passives tend to be dull. The normal structure of that noble English sentence Churchill talked about is *Subject–transitive verb–direct object.* The information flows forward as the reader reads, from subject to object; and the action word, or the locomotive pulling that information forward, is the verb. This is the structure served by the active voice verb. In the passive voice, with the subject receiving the action of the verb rather than performing it, that flow to the reader is backward. It's inartistic. No novelist would write: *Their glasses were smashed into the fireplace, each of them was passionately embraced by the other, and a warm throbbing was felt as each of their bodies was pressed against the other.* So, you see, even when the passive serves a useful purpose, it's dull—yet another reason good writers keep most of their verbs in the active voice.

Caution: ***passive*** **and** ***past*** **are not the same.** They sound somewhat alike only by accident. Do not assume that all passive voice verbs are in the past tense. Passives occur in all tenses. We could say: *The proposal was approved. . . . The proposal is being approved. . . .* or *The proposal will be approved.* There you have past, present, and future tenses. But they are all passive voice verbs.

What about contractions?

They're never necessary; you can achieve a relaxed, informal tone without them. But an occasional one is acceptable in all but the most formal writing. Simply don't overdo the privilege.

The first contraction in this book appears near the end of paragraph 2, page 8.

For the language gourmet

What's the difference between a gourmet and a gourmand?

A gourmet is a judge of good food. A gourmand is a person who overeats.

Passives are easy to recognize and to turn active. They all have some form of the verb *to be* in front of the main verb. *The proposal **was** approved. The statement **must be** updated. Mary **is** loved.* After you have recognized it, turning it active is simple. Just ask yourself *By whom?* The answer to that question gives you the subject you need for an active voice sentence:

It is recommended that we make the changes. By whom? *The Atlanta office recommends that we make the changes.* Or, *I recommend that we make the changes. The glasses were smashed into the fireplace . . . .* By whom? *They smashed the glasses* (subject–transitive verb–direct object) . . . .

THAT vs. WHICH?

Let's settle this question once and for all. The answer is easy.

Use *that* when the clause it introduces is *restrictive*; use *which* when it is *nonrestrictive*. (See pages 38 and 39.) Thus: *The car with snow tires was the only one that got up the hill.* But: *The blue car, which had snow tires, was the only one that . . . .*

And while we're at it, what in grammar is a *WHICH HUNT?* It's an attempt, usually by a careful editor, to change *which* to *that* when careless writers don't know the difference.

By the way, careful writers know something else interesting about *that:* Even when it's used the correct grammatical way, it's often wasted. You can often drop it and not miss it: *I think that the report goes into too much detail.* Now try: *I think the report goes into too much detail.* The meaning is identical, but one less word means the pace is a bit faster and more interesting. BUT NOTE: *I believe that Melissa should help on this project.* Without *that*, readers might turn the wrong direction: *I believe Melissa . . .* (having to do with her credibility). A useful habit: Every time you write *that*, try reading the sentence without it; you may decide to drop it about half the time.

Exercise 17:

Rewrite each of the following sentences from the passive to the active voice. Circle every verb. Underline its subject, and double-underline its object:

17-1. More than 7,000 cigarettes a year are consumed by a pack-a-day smoker.

_____

17-2. As quickly as bits of their sandwiches were dropped by the picnickers, they were snatched from the sand by hungry seagulls.

_____

_____

17-3. An average of 23 percent more is spent by American shoppers when credit cards are used than when cash is paid.

_____

_____

17-4. The smell of fresh-cut grass had never before been known by most of these kids.

_____

17-5. (_From a Bagby Research Institute scientific report._)
Detailed experiments to measure resiliency of polystyrene foam were conducted in 1979, and their results were re-evaluated last year.

_____

_____

_____

Exercise 17.

Each of the following sentences is now in the active voice. The verbs are circled. Their subjects are underlined, and their objects are double-underlined. Notice that subjects and objects have traded places. (The second and third sentences of this introductory paragraph are in the *passive* voice—for an important reason: *By whom* is obvious and would be a distraction if included.)

17-1. A pack-a-day smoker (consumes) more than 7,000 cigarettes a year. Page 90.

17-2. *Two passive constructions changed:* As quickly as the picnickers (dropped) bits of their sandwiches, hungry seagulls (snatched) them from the sand. Page 90.

17-3. *Three passive constructions changed:* American shoppers (spend) an average of 23 percent more when they (use) credit cards than when they (pay) cash. Page 90.

17-4. Most of these kids (had) never before (known) the smell of fresh-cut grass. Page 90.

17-5. PLEASE READ CAREFULLY. *You couldn't possibly know this*:

Klodele Chemical Company, Geneva, Switzerland, (conducted) detailed experiments to measure resiliency of polystyrene foam in 1979, and Bagby Research Institute (re-evaluated) their results last year. Page 90.

NOTE: The conditions in the original sentence may have been the most dangerous possible for passive voice verbs. Two unidentified actions are from different sources, and some background information tempts (perhaps encourages) readers to match them incorrectly. (Remember, the statement was in a Bagby Research Institute report.) Readers would almost inevitably read: *Bagby Research Institute conducted . . . , and we re-evaluated the results last year.* This is a misinterpretation that almost had to happen; the writer set it up. Yet the *writer* usually doesn't see anything wrong with a sentence like the original. (He or she knows who did what, and isn't relying on the little black marks on the page to find out.)

The Five Taboos

The Five Taboos

For the grammar gourmet:

Two English teachers were comparing trips. One asked, "Did you get scrod in Boston?" The other hesitantly replied, "Well, yes, but I never heard it called by the plus-perfect participle before."

(Pronounced "plew" or "ploo." It's the same as past-perfect participle.)

As you passed through our education system, some English teachers (or teachers of other subjects who saw fit to comment on writing style) may have given you some **bad** advice on writing. Theodore Bernstein, author of several books on writing, called everybody's English teacher "Miss Thistlebottom," and she was the archtypical troublemaker. Has any teacher ever encouraged you to use the largest words you can, or to construct the longest sentences you can?

The influence that causes such mistaken beliefs may have been literature, because much of English literature from past centuries is certainly hard to read. What the teacher did not tell you, however, is that the English language has changed drastically since most literature was written. (See pages 16 and 28.) Also, the style of writing that is often referred to as 'literary style' was often an attempt to use language as a communications barrier, not a communications tool. In past centuries many educated people wrote deliberately in a heavy style so their writing could be understood only by others like themselves. Heavy writing became fashionable; it became the mark of the intellectual, and gradually, much of academic writing became almost impossible for non-academic people to understand. At about that same time, English teachers had gradually become specialists at explaining literature from earlier periods. Most still are. *And they continue to encourage literary or academic style as the model of how you should write today*.

Still, here and there you surely learned many useful things about language usage. Unfortunately, most people also receive some harmful pieces of advice along the way. The harmful ones are usually negative—things you were told you *may not* do. Five in particular are so widespread almost everybody has been exposed to them. You probably learned them as rules of grammar, or rules of composition. But these five are not rules and never have been. Let us expose them and get rid of them forever.

TABOO NO. 1—*THAT YOU MAY NOT BEGIN A SENTENCE WITH 'AND' OR 'BUT'*. Of course you may. In fact, there are times you should. Here is why:

These words are conjunctions, or *connectives*. They connect your ideas, and the basic vehicle of the idea is *the sentence*. When the English teacher tells you that you may not begin sentences with *And* or *But*, you are deprived of the two most useful words for connecting sentences smoothly. Two choices remain: You may have the smooth flow of the connective **or** the clarity and efficiency of short sentences, but not both.

But good writers refuse to make that choice. They insist on the right to have the smooth, logical flow of the connectives **and** the clarity and efficiency of short sentences. So should you. Otherwise you are left with two poor choices: long smooth sentences or short choppy ones. What can be wrong with short smooth ones?

Of course, do not go out of your way to begin sentences with *And* or *But*; rather, do not back off from doing so when it seems the natural thing to do. Here is an example in which a splendid writer felt it was natural and desirable to begin sentences with *And* and *But*. It is from *The Wall Street Journal*, regularly one of the best written publications in the United States:

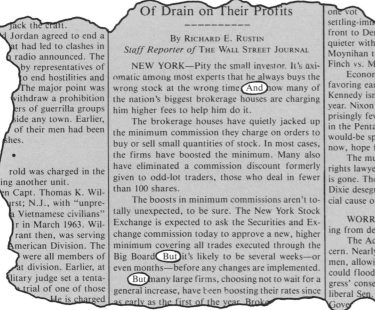

—*The Wall Street Journal*

You may be thinking, "The Wall Street Journal has literary freedom to bend the rules of grammar." But (oops!) there has never been a rule against beginning sentences with *And* or *But*. Witness this passage from *The Oxford English Dictionary*, acknowledged by scholars worldwide to be the most respected authority on English language usage:

GENERAL EXPLANATIONS.

THE VOCABULARY.

THE Vocabulary of a widely-diffused and highly-cultivated living language is not a fixed quantity circumscribed by definite limits. That vast aggregate of words and phrases which constitutes the Vocabulary of English-speaking men presents, to the mind that endeavours to grasp it as a definite whole, the aspect of one of those nebulous masses familiar to the astronomer, in which a clear and unmistakable nucleus shades off on all sides, through zones of decreasing brightness, to a dim marginal film that seems to end nowhere, but to lose itself imperceptibly in the surrounding darkness. In its constitution it may be compared to one of those natural groups of the zoologist or botanist, wherein typical species forming the characteristic nucleus of the order, are linked on every side to other species, in which the typical character is less and less distinctly apparent, till it fades away in an outer fringe of aberrant forms, which merge imperceptibly in various surrounding orders, and whose own position is ambiguous and uncertain. For the convenience of classification, the naturalist may draw the line, which bounds a class or order, outside or inside of a particular form; but Nature has drawn it nowhere. So the English Vocabulary contains a nucleus or central mass of many thousand words whose 'Anglicity' is unquestioned; some of them only literary, some of them only colloquial, the great majority at once literary and colloquial,—they are the *Common Words* of the language. But they are linked on every side with other words which are less and less entitled to this appellation, and which pertain ever more and more distinctly to the domain of local dialect, of the slang and cant of 'sets' and classes, of the peculiar technicalities of trades and processes, of the scientific terminology common to all civilized nations, of the actual languages of other lands and peoples. And there is absolutely no defining line in any direction: the circle of the English language has a well-defined centre but no discernible circumference*. Yet practical utility has some bounds, and a Dictionary has definite limits: The lexicographer must, like the naturalist, 'draw the line somewhere', in each direction. He must include all the 'Common Words' and scientific, tec...

—*Oxford University Press*

Conjunctions vs. Conjunctive adverbs: The difference

Adverbs that serve as conjunctions save writers some awkward moments. If you are among those who believe it's improper to begin sentences with *and* or *but* (see page 96) and will not yield, you can use *also* or *however* and still have sentences of reasonable length joined smoothly by connectives.

Skillful writers like conjunctive adverbs, however, for yet another reason. Because these connectives are adverbs, not conjunctions, they modify the verb. You get the choice, therefore, of placing them at the beginning of the main clause or in the middle (as in this one).

Among the most useful words in English are such connectives as: *furthermore, however, incidentally, likewise, nevertheless, otherwise*, and *therefore*. These are all adverbs, not conjunctions.

Separate a conjunctive adverb from the rest of the sentence by commas—one comma if it's at the beginning or end, two if it's in the middle. (See page 63.)

Talk about ending with prepositions . . .

The child asked the parent: *What did you bring a book I didn't want to be read to out of up for?*

What's the singular of parentheses?

It's parenthesis, but you should never need to use this, unless you have left one out. (See page 64.)

The odd thing about this taboo is that all of us read sentences every day beginning with *And* and *But*. You can surely find them, almost at random, in almost any good book you may be reading today. But you have probably never noticed them. And that, incidentally, should be a clue to you that if you use them intelligently your readers will not notice either when you begin sentences with the two most useful connectives in the English language.

As a matter of fact, if you are part of the ever-growing group of writers who believe that short sentences improve readability (see page 51), you will find that the connectives are particularly important to your writing. They are bridges between ideas. True, as the English teacher says, they add nothing to the grammar. But they do add important smoothness, by providing continuity. There is logical meaning imparted by that word *And*. Subconsciously, the reader receives: *The next idea is related to and agrees with the last one.* Still a different logical meaning imparted by *But*: (*The next idea is related to but contradicts the last one.*) Other connectives are equally important. Look for opportunities to begin sentences with words like *Therefore* (*The next idea is related to and the result of the last one.*), *Next, Nevertheless*, and many others. Do not deprive yourself of these important *bridges of thoughts*.

Remember, you, the writer, can *feel* the logical relationships between those thoughts. But readers are paper readers, not mind readers. They must *see* those relationships, and you must put the words there that will allow them to do so.

TABOO NO. 2 is at the ends of sentences—*THAT YOU MAY NOT END A SENTENCE WITH A PREPOSITION*. Of course you may. The alternative may be an awkward, unnatural sentence. We admit that prepositions are weak words; therefore, when a sentence ends with one it tends to dribble to a close rather than ending crisply. Still, that is sometimes a better alternative than taking the long way around.

Perhaps the best known illustration of this point is a famous Winston Churchill story. Allegedly he was criticized for ending a sentence with a preposition, and he shot back: "*This is the type of arrant pedantry up with which I will not put.*" There you have the awkward, unnatural sentence as an alternative to ending with a preposition. If the story is true, Churchill (author of the five-volume *A History of the English-Speaking Peoples*) would end with two prepositions.

The prejudice against ending sentences with prepositions seems to come, in some fuzzy way, from Latin. Fuzzy because Latin has no such restriction. (In fact, perhaps the most widely used phrase in the history of Western civilization is the liturgical, *Dominus vobiscum*. That's "God be with you," and notice where the *cum* [*with*] is located.)

Even if Latin had such a restriction, however, to proclaim that it must therefore apply to English would be a non sequitur. Ours is not one of the Romance languages (see page 18), and Latin rules simply do not fit the Anglo Saxon mold.

Another unsound preposition argument is that the word *pre-position* means it must be placed in front of something—presumably its object. Then there is the theory that a preposition at the end of a sentence is technically not a preposition but an adverb (modifying the verb). We'll leave that for the grammatical scholars to struggle with.

TABOO NO. 3 is probably the most damaging of all—*THAT YOU MAY NOT REPEAT WORDS*. Let's not call a spade a gardening implement. The teacher probably told you, "Use a word once. If you need it again, or at least if you need it very soon, that's too bad. You've used it up. You should find a synonym instead." That is terrible advice!

The issue here is *first-choice words*. When an intelligent adult uses a particular word—either intuitively or after careful thought to keep the writing clear—this is probably endorsement that it was the first-choice word for that situation.

"Seek other words to add variety to your writing," the teacher may have told you. But our objectives are clarity and precision—not variety. If your first-choice word was the correct one, but now you are forced to use something else, you go to a second-, third-, then fourth-choice word. That's too high a price to pay. Rather, re-use your first-choice word.

Because of its hodge-podge history (see page 14), English offers more synonyms than most other languages. But there are few *exact* synonyms—even in English; you usually go from specific to abstract when you seek them. From *automobile* to *vehicle*, for example. But the abstract word may offer a choice of several specific meanings (a vehicle can be many other things). Therefore, the writing becomes less precise; the writer (sender) loses control of what the reader (receiver) receives.

Or, you may **mislead** the reader by switching words. He or she may not realize you intended the two words to mean the same thing. For example, suppose you are writing about a warehouse. If you cannot use the word *warehouse* again, you might refer to it as the *facility* the second time. And the third time you might refer to it as the *unit*. Later, you also refer to something else as *the unit*.

That, incidentally, is probably the most misused word in business writing. Use *unit* only when you are referring to units of measure, such as unit price or unit package. Do not use *unit* as a universal synonym. (An advertisement for an apartment building says: *The unit contains 232 units*.) Used that way, a unit is an industrial *whatchama-callit*.

In journalism, the tendency to seek synonyms is often referred to as *the elongated yellow fruit syndrome*, in derision of writers who would not be caught calling a banana a banana twice. Such writers, of course, refer to money (the second time) as *that elusive green stuff* and to snow as *that cold white stuff*. If that's what English teachers mean when they refer to "variety," let's have none of it.

By all means, repeat first-choice words. Remember, your objectives when choosing words should be clarity and precision—not variety. When you use second-, third-, or fourth-choice words, you are hurting your reader.

To avoid too much repetition, the language gives us pronouns. You can refer to the warehouse as *it*, or to two or more warehouses as *they*. Of course, you may do this only after establishing what *it* or *they* stands for by using the original word, the antecedent of the pronoun, first (see page 76). Use pronouns as naturally in your writing as you would in conversation.

TABOO NO. 4—*THAT YOU MAY NOT SWITCH VERB TENSES*. Unthinkable advice. How else would one say: *The President has announced that several turkeys received as Thanksgiving gifts, which are now residing happily on White House grounds, will be given to organizations for needy children*. OR: *I have studied* (past) *your plan carefully, and I think* (present) *it will be* (future) *very helpful*.

It's hard to guess what the teacher had in mind in giving anyone this advice, but many people learn at some point in their lives—and honestly believe—that they may not mix verb tenses. The exact details are vague; most people who believe this say the limitation applies only within a given sentence, but some actually have the notion that the tense of the first verb is supposed to lock the writer into that tense for the rest of that piece of writing.

Perhaps there's some merit in telling children: Don't mix verbs of different tense when the actions they describe all happen in the same tense. (*I ran, then he runs, then I ran again* . . .) But that's simply saying: Be careful to use verbs correctly. If the advice is, *Don't mix verb tenses incorrectly*, we can live with it.

TABOO NO. 5. While we are disposing of rules that are not really rules, let's get rid of one that is not on grammar but on composition—*THAT YOU MAY NOT WRITE A ONE-SENTENCE PARAGRAPH*.

A topic sentence for every paragraph?

That's another taboo worth forgetting.

Opening every paragraph with a topic sentence is a good idea *if you can do it conveniently*. Readers like summary information in advance; they're better able, then, to read and assimilate the details. (A topic sentence at the beginning of *every* paragraph also helps speedreaders; they can read just those sentences and still get most of the important information.)

Still, to *require* a topic sentence at the beginning of every paragraph would be far too rigid a discipline. Most skilled writers simply can't write that way and don't try.

WHO or WHOM?

Which is correct? To tell, you've got to be able to recognize whether it's being used as a subject or an object. *Who* is nominative (for subjects), and *whom* is objective (for objects).

Sometimes it's easy to tell: *Who* (subject) *took this photograph? Whom* (object) *should the letter be addressed to?** But other times you may have to examine carefully: *The receipt must be signed by (whoever or whomever?) receives the package.* Answer: *whoever*, because it's the subject of the clause, *whoever receives the package.* (The entire clause is the object of the preposition *by.*)

By the way, the possessive of *who* is *whose*, not *who's.* Use *who's* only as the contraction of *who is.*

*Yes, you may end a sentence with a preposition. (See page 98.) If doing so bothers you, however, write: *To whom should the letter be addressed.* Either way, *whom* is the object of the preposition *to.*

The rationale here, many English teachers argue, is that a paragraph is a group of related sentences. Then, who ever heard of a group of one?

Undeniably, the clustering of related ideas into paragraphs helps readers. A paragraph *is* a cluster of related sentences, and in that sense it is an important tool in establishing the logical relationships between written ideas. And, reading experts tell us, the paragraph *break* provides readers an important aid in assimilating as they read. That break announces: Stop here and regroup the thoughts if you wish; a new idea is coming. And readers do just that—intuitively. Suppose, though, a new idea comes after just one sentence. What then of the "cluster paragraph" theory?

We must allow the occasional cluster of one.

In fact, writers using paragraph structure to help readers will occasionally put a very important idea into an ultra-short paragraph—sometimes as short as a few words—for yet another reason: It stands out from the rest, jumping off the page so that even scanning readers can't miss it. (See the one above.)

But caution: Don't write short, one-sentence paragraphs very often. Again, it is true that, generally speaking, a paragraph is a cluster of related sentences. In that sense the paragraph is one of the important tools of logic in writing. If your paragraphs are too short, or too long, your logic will disintegrate before your reader's eyes.

Exercise 18:

Improve each of these passages by making a change described as one of _The Five Taboos_. Try not to make any other changes:

18-1. Most snakes are not poisonous. Most people think they are, and the resulting caution causes many useful snakes to be killed.

_____

_____

18-2. We must know from which office this package came.

_____

18-3. Ice cream is not an American invention. Many Europeans describe its use in aristocratic dining rooms centuries ago, and historians credit Nero with serving the cold dessert during the Roman Empire.

_____

_____

_____

18-4. The photography magazines say color printing is easy. Being a good amateur photographer, and particularly in darkroom techniques, I decided to try. So I bought all the necessary items, and many that are not necessary but nice to have—like an expensive color analyzer. Nothing could stop me.

   Color printing is the hardest thing I have ever tried to do in photography. Somehow, things do not happen for me the way the articles and ads promise they will. In black and white printing, I know how to control the variables to achieve exactly the effect I want. In color, I have no feelings for the effects that exposure and development have on the print. Therefore, I cannot predict the results, and I am not in control. I get a few good prints, but through trial and error rather than skill.

_____

_____

_____

_____

_____

_____

_____

_____

_____

_____

18-5. The Declaration of Independence is dated July 4, 1776, but the official declaration was made July 2, and the signing took place August 2.

_____

_____

18-6. I don't like to fight. But I would rather engage in hostilities than give in on an important point and be sorry later.

_____

_____

18-7. Keep your MegaMower's engine clean. Like all power units, it requires air for combustion and cooling, and dirt and foreign particles are its enemies.

_____

_____

18-8. For most of us the Freedom of Information Act means we can watch the government watch us. It means we can find out what the government has found out about us. While it doesn't prevent prying officials from snooping and violating our rights, it makes it harder for them to do so.

_____

_____

_____

_____

18-9. Not one of us has the slightest idea of the nature of your complaint.

_____

18-10. Since the People's Republic of China began attracting American tourists in 1979 (Europeans were welcomed much earlier), some remarkable changes have taken place there. Luxury hotels, shops, and restaurants are springing up in major cities. And the government tourist bureau, once guided by the view that visitors had to receive an education, now seems to accept that vacations for fun are okay. While many first-wave tourists complained of spartan accommodations and arduous schedules, many Americans now are coming back from China reporting fun experiences. You should not go to China, however, with the notion you will come back a Sinologist after your stint of a few weeks.

For one thing, the land is so immense you cannot possibly see a cross-section in your three or four weeks. (Imagine a group of Chinese touring New York, Washington D.C.,

Chicago, and Los Angeles and presuming they know all about the U.S.) For another, the cultures are so different from ours that outsiders who have spent years there don't pretend to understand them fully. Still, you should go to China if you can.

_____

_____

_____

_____

_____

_____

_____

_____

_____

_____

_____

_____

_____

_____

Self-Study Exercises

(Answer Key: pages 104 and 105)

Exercise 18.

Each of the passages has been improved by making a change described as one of *The Five Taboos*. **No other changes have been made. Changes are italicized:**

18-1. Most snakes are not poisonous. *But* most people think they are, and the resulting caution causes many useful snakes to be killed. Page 96.

18-2. We must know which office this package came *from*. Page 98.

18-3. Ice cream is not an American invention. Many Europeans describe its use in aristocratic dining rooms centuries ago, and historians credit Nero with serving *ice cream* during the Roman Empire. Page 98.

18-4. *Notice the effect an occasional one-sentence paragraph can create.* (Page 99.) *The only change here is that the first sentence of the second paragraph is made a separate paragraph:*

The photography magazines say color printing is easy. Being a good amateur photographer, and particularly in darkroom techniques, I decided to try. So I bought all the necessary items, and many that are not necessary but nice to have—like an expensive color analyzer. Nothing could stop me.

Color printing is the hardest thing I have ever tried to do in photography.

Somehow, things do not happen for me the way the articles and ads promise they will. In black and white printing, I know how to control the variables to achieve exactly the effect I want. In color, I have no feelings for the effects that exposure and development have on the print. Therefore, I cannot predict the results, and I am not in control. I get a few good prints, but through trial and error rather than skill.

18-5. The Declaration of Independence is dated July 4, 1776. *But* the official declaration was made July 2, and the signing took place August 2. Page 96.

18-6. I don't like to fight. But I would rather *fight* than give in on an important point and be sorry later. Page 98.

18-7. Keep your MegaMower's engine clean. Like all *engines*, it requires air for combustion and cooling, and dirt and foreign particles are its enemies. Page 98. (Note that the abstract term *power units*, used in the original as a synonym, is not an exact synonym; as a result the original passage is technically inaccurate. [Internal combustion engines need air, but not all power units do.])

18-8. For most of us, the Freedom of Information Act means we can watch the government watch us. It means we can find out what the government has found out about us. *And,* while it doesn't prevent prying officials from snooping and violating our rights, it makes it harder for them to do so. Page 96.

18-9. Not one of us has the slightest idea what your complaint is *about*. Page 98.

18-10. *Again, an occasional one-sentence paragraph allows the writer to make important ideas stand out.* (Page 99.) *The only changes here are that the last sentence of each paragraph is made a separate paragraph. What a difference in the flow of information as the reader assimilates it:*

Since the People's Republic of China began attracting American tourists in 1979 (Europeans were welcomed much earlier), some remarkable changes have taken place there. Luxury hotels, shops, and restaurants are springing up in major cities. And the government tourist bureau, once guided by the view that visitors had to receive an education, now seems to accept that vacations for fun are okay. While many first-wave tourists complained of spartan accommodations and arduous schedules, many Americans now are coming back from China reporting fun experiences.

You should not go to China, however, with the notion you will come back a Sinologist after your stint of a few weeks.

For one thing, the land is so immense you cannot possibly see a cross-section in your three or four weeks. (Imagine a group of Chinese touring New York, Washington D.C., Chicago, and Los Angeles and presuming they know all about the U.S.) For another, the cultures are so different from ours that outsiders who have spent years there don't pretend to understand them fully.

Still, you should go to China if you can.

Linguistic Limerick

In syntax, the lost preposition
Confounds every writer's ambition.
Does astute placement tend
Toward the front or the end?
The answer defies erudition.

(A. J.)

Guidelines
for
Nonsexist
Writing

Guidelines for Nonsexist Writing

How formal should you be?

Language is much like clothing in two important ways: Both are highly visible; and in both, different styles are appropriate for different situations.

In clothing, jeans and T-shirts serve an important purpose; so do formal gowns and tuxedos. These are extremes, however; for the office, you need something more moderate.

Likewise, moderate language is the most appropriate in the office—or in almost any writing situation, for that matter. Many writers try to sound too formal. Perhaps they're trying to impress, and perhaps for the same reason that so many writers try to sound as scholarly as possible. (See pages 14 and 28.)

Few people would write: *Cool the groady greens*

Avoiding sexist language is not only morally correct, it is easy. In some writing, it is also the law.

English is notoriously sexist—more so than any other major language, according to language scholars. Still, it is possible to write **anything** without sexist references of any kind, if you are willing. Furthermore, doing so should not make your writing any more difficult, and it need not create the least bit of awkward wording.

The infamous generic *he*.

This is, of course, the most common abuse. For years business people have written statements like: *The customer might not be aware he may request this service.* Unthinkable today. So you write: *The customer might not be aware he/she may request this service.* At least, it will avoid complaints from your customers and your employees. But it is awkward. It calls attention to itself, especially if you do it often.

One simple change will get rid of three quarters of those sexist statements—graciously. *He* and *she* are **third person** pronouns. English simply does not have neutral personal pronouns **in the third person singular.** Switch, then, to **plural:** *Customers might not be aware they may request . . . .* Or, switch to second person: *You might not be aware . . . .* (You should do that anyhow, where it fits, in writing that addresses the reader directly. Your writing will be warmer, a desirable trait.)

That type of change will usually work, but not always. For example, in a memo to supervisors you might write: *The supervisor must inform an employee as soon as he or she is suspected of drug abuse that he or she may face disciplinary action.* Second person (*you . . . that you may face*) or third person plural (*employees . . . that they may face*) will not work here, so you must use the *he or she*—even if the sentence requires it twice, as here. This usage is awkward only if you use it repeatedly. And use *he or she* rather than *he/she*. It sounds better to the mind's ear.

Job descriptions, one of the curses of anybody who has ever tried to write them, are a bit harder to keep nonsexist, but still not very hard. Here, more than in most other kinds of writing, old-fashioned (sexist) language habits are an invitation to legal difficulties. Federal courts have ruled that all-male policy statements, even though unintentional, are discriminatory, and some companies have been hurt by resulting law suits.

The problem in job descriptions is that you are writing a series of required skills or duties (or both) for *any* employee who holds that particular job, and each sentence tends to have a pronoun (traditionally *he*) as its subject:

> *The (job title) must be capable of reading and understanding blueprints according to NA level 6 specifications. He must be capable of making bookkeeping entries and preparing financial statements in NCPA format. He must . . . . He must . . . .*

Unacceptable. That invites Equal Employment Opportunity grievances. *You* or *they* will not work here. Using *he or she* each time will quickly become distracting, and the style awkward. Combining several statements into fewer longer sentences would mean fewer subjects, therefore fewer sexist/nonsexist word choices. But such sentences quickly become too long and complex to follow.

Solution: Write each section of a job description as a series of phrases, without subjects. This can be done in correct grammar and in smooth, gracious style. For each section, an introductory phrase contains the subject; this is followed by a series of sentence fragments, each without a subject, each telling one of the requirements. Example:

The (job title) must be capable of:
- *—Reading and understanding blueprints according to NA level 6 specifications.*
- *—Making bookkeeping entries and preparing financial statements in NCPA format.*

Be sure to list the ideas vertically, indented, as they are here. That way they can be read separately, rather than as one unbearably long sentence, even though grammatically they are still one sentence. Changes of this kind are easy and will avoid Equal Employment Opportunity grievances. Caution: this format can tend to sound choppy and fragmented; therefore, take extra care to be smooth.

Other *man* words.

With equal ease you can get rid of all other *man* words. They are never, never necessary. *Man is a social animal . . .* would be better as, *People are social animals.* Anthropologically, both statements say exactly the same thing. *Since the beginning of mankind . . .* would be better as, *Since earliest human history . . . .* In both cases, the nonsexist version is clear, gracious, and just as accurate.

Male bosses and female secretaries?

That may indeed be the situation in most offices, but you must not portray it that way in your writing. You lose no effectiveness whatever in an interoffice memo or letter by writing, *Every executive must be aware of his or her responsibilities . . . .* Or, of course, *Every secretary must be aware of his or her . . . .* Incredibly, the National Council for Teachers of English (NCTE) recommends *. . . must be aware of their . . . .* That is terrible grammar, however (singular noun, plural pronoun), and unnecessary. (See page 75.) Once poor grammar is endorsed for special situations, where does it stop? Who decides if a situation is special enough? This academic permissiveness is an invitation to the "anything goes" attitude in language usage. Some NCTE committees endorse that attitude.

Avoid job titles that identify sex. *Mailmen* have become *mail carriers. Salesmen* are *sales representatives.* In airplanes, *stewardesses* have become *flight attendants.* Likewise, if you are seriously interested in finding nonsexist descriptions in your writing, you surely can without much effort.

What about *chairman*? No mystery. Use *chairman* for males, *chairwoman* for females. If it is a theoretical one, use *presiding officer,* or *committee head,* or even *person in charge.* Please do **not** use the grossly distasteful "chair," which is also recommended by NCTE.

Never refer to a grown woman as a girl. *The girl who took the order . . .* will get you icy stares, and should. *The woman who took the order . . .* is far more thoughtful. Also, never refer to women as *ladies.* The word is judgmental, and people who care about these matters insist such judgment is not necessary.

About *Ms.*

Yes, you should use it in addressing all women—single or married. We do not have different forms of *Mr.* for single and married men. According to surveys, the word *Ms.* (pronounced *mizz*) has slowly but consistently gained in popularity. By the late 1970's, the majority of professional women favored it, and most publishers' style manuals endorsed it. (*The USGPO Style Manual,* however, has stayed mum on this subject. *The Chicago Manual of Style* acknowledges the use of *Ms.* but does not encourage or discourage its use.)

around the pad, instead of *Please kill the weeds around the building.* But many would write: *Attention should be addressed to the necessity of eliminating undesirable vegetation surrounding the periphery of our facility,* and that's equally inappropriate. Worse, it fails to communicate. In fact, such over-complicated writing often causes mistakes through misinterpretation.

What about the beauty of language? Any poet will tell you it's the small words, not the large ones, that give writing a sense of rhythm and imagery.

What about dignity? It comes from your *ideas*, not the words and sentences used to convey them. If your ideas are dignified, they will lose nothing by being conveyed in plain English. In fact, they will gain by becoming visible to more people.

Exercise 19:

Rewrite each of the following sentences to eliminate sexist references, yet keeping the style as gracious as possible:

19-1. When writing is unclear, the reader may not be aware he misunderstood.

_____

19-2. The girl in our sales department who takes your order will also arrange for delivery.

_____

19-3. A policeman who gives you a ticket is not required to tell you his name.

_____

19-4. Beth, a cocktail waitress, believes that a waiter or waitress should not have to pay income tax on his or her tips.

_____

_____

19-5. Ida Feldman will be chairman next year.

_____

19-6. Each employee is responsible for keeping their work area neat and clean.

_____

19-7. A nurse must constantly take training programs, to keep her knowledge of her profession up to date.

_____

_____

19-8. Man is the only animal that cries.

_____

19-9. When a new boss takes over, he should try to meet with the employees and explain any special expectations he may have.

_____

_____

19-10. If you expect a secretary to correct your spelling, tell her so.

_____

Self-Study Exercise

(Answer Key: page 112)

Exercise 19.

Each of these sentences is rewritten to eliminate sexist references. With a little thought, it is possible to be nonsexist without sounding awkward. The changes are italicized:

19-1. When writing is unclear, readers may not be aware *they* misunderstood. Page 108.

19-2. The *woman* in our sales department who takes your order will also arrange for delivery. Page 109.

19-3. A police *officer* who gives you a ticket is not required to tell you *his or her* name. (The *he or she* usage doesn't call attention to itself unless you overdo it.) Page 108.

19-4. Beth, a cocktail waitress, believes that waiters or waitresses should not have to pay income tax on *their* tips. OR: . . . *on tips.* Page 108.

19-5. Ida Feldman will be *chairwoman* next year. Page 109.

19-6. Each employee is responsible for keeping *his or her* work area neat and clean. (Not even in the name of nonsexism may you use pronouns that don't agree in number with their nouns.) Pages 75 and 109.

19-7. *Nurses* must constantly take training programs, to keep *their* knowledge of *their* profession up to date. Page 108.

19-8. *People* are the only animals that cry. Page 109.

19-9. When taking over, a new boss should try to meet with the employees and explain any special expectations *he or she* may have. OR: When *you* take over as a new boss, *you* should try . . . . Page 109.

19-10. If you expect *secretaries* to correct your spelling, tell *them* so. Page 108.

Spelling Tips

Spelling Tips

For most of us, correct spelling doesn't come easy. If your language were Spanish, it might be considerably easier, because in Spanish, more than in any other major language, things are spelled the way they sound. English is the opposite extreme; of all the major languages, linguists tell us, English is the most irregular and inconsistent—in both spelling and punctuation. (See "About English," page 14.)

But the irregular words are a tiny minority. By far the majority of our words *do* follow a few simple rules; most of us simply never learn them.

Before those rules, however, this advice: If you're having trouble spelling a word, try taking it apart in your mind. Examine the parts for small words you already know how to spell, or for prefixes (added to the beginning of words) or suffixes (added to the end). Surprisingly often, if you can break a word into smaller parts this way you will recognize the parts. Take, for example, the word *prefix. Pre* means *before*, and we all know what *fix* means; literally, then, prefix means *something you fix onto the beginning of a word.* Or take *vegetable. Veg* comes from *vegetation; et* relates to *eat*; and we all know what *able* means. Now examine *unpredictability*. Break it down the same way; find the parts that the word is made of, and often they'll be easy to spell.

And this caution: Sometimes no logic can explain the spelling of a word. Hence: veg*etables* are *edible*. Ah, well. Keep a spelling dictionary handy, and use it whenever you feel the slightest uncertainty.

Now, a few simple and (usually) reliable rules.

1. When a **prefix** is added to a word, the spelling of the original word does not change (*anti + aircraft = antiaircraft*). If the prefix ends with the same letter the original word begins with (*in + numerable, dis + similar*), don't drop one of the letters; keep the double letter (*innumerable, dissimilar*).

The same is true for **suffixes** (*literal + ly = literally; stubborn + ness = stubbornness*).

2. If a word ends with a consonant followed by a silent *e* (*note, drive*), drop the *e* when you add any suffix that begins with a vowel (*notable, driving*). BUT NOT if the suffix begins with a consonant (*late, lateness; manage, management*). (NOTE, however: *changeable, judgment.*)

3. If a one-syllable word ends with a consonant preceded by a vowel, (*big, stop, wet*), double the consonant when you add any suffix that begins with a vowel (*biggest, stopping, wettable*). BUT NOT if the word contains a double vowel (*nearer, weeping*) or ends with two consonants (*longest, burnable*), or the suffix begins with a consonant (*thinly, bagful*).

Double the last consonant also on a word having more than one syllable if the accent is on the last syllable (*begin, beginning; regret, regrettable*). (BUT NOT: *profit, profitable* [*because the accent is on the first syllable*]).

4. If a *verb* ends with a *y* preceded by a consonant (*fly, accompany*), keep the *y* when adding *ing* (*flying, accompanying*). But change the *y* to *i* when adding *es* or *ed* (*flies, accompanied*). NOTE: This rule applies also to *nouns*, but the explanation differs slightly: Change the *y* to *ie* before adding *s* to make a noun plural (*battery, batteries; delivery, deliveries*).

Should you spell numbers?

The basic rule is simple. Spell out one-digit numbers (one through nine); use numerals for all numbers having two or more digits.

There are some exceptions, but they are logical and simple. Use numerals for all numbers in dates, for street addresses, and for enumerations (such as paragraph numbers) no matter how low or high. Also, use numerals for *all* numbers in a sentence that contains both kinds (209 people for 5 jobs); the idea here is to be consistent *within any sentence.*

-sede, -ceed, or -cede?

Only one word ends with *sede: supersede*. Only three words end with *ceed; exceed, proceed, and succeed.* All others end with *cede (intercede, precede).*

5. For *ie* or *ei* when pronounced like *ee* (as in *keep*), remember this verse: Put *i* before *e*, except after *c* (*believe, yield*, but *ceiling, receive*). (There are exceptions to this rule, however: *neither, weird, financier*.)

6. To form plurals of nouns, just add *s* to most words. But: If a noun ends with *s*, or an *s* sound (*sh, ch, x,* or *z*), add *es* to make it plural (*surplus, surpluses; dish, dishes; bench, benches; box, boxes; waltz, waltzes*).

Other rules for plurals:

If a noun ends with *f* (*half, leaf*), change the *f* to *ve* when adding *s* to make it plural (*halves, leaves*). If the noun ends with *fe* (*knife, wife*), just change the *f* to *v* (the *e* is already there) when adding the *s*. NOTE, however: There are exceptions, but they're sensible. If the *ves* ending would cause the plural noun to look like a verb (*proof, proves; safe, saves*), leave the *f* to make it plural (*proof, proofs; safe, safes*). If a noun ends with *ff* (*cliff, staff*), make it plural the conventional way, just by adding *s* (*cliffs, staffs*).

If a noun ends with *y* preceded by a consonant (*city, company, spy*), change the *y* to *ie* when adding *s* to make it plural (*cities, companies, spies*). (See 4 [page 114].) If the *y* is preceded by a vowel (*journey, play*), make it plural the conventional way, just by adding *s* (*journeys, plays*).

If a noun ends with *o* preceded by a consonant (*hero, potato and tomato*), add *es* to make it plural (*heroes, potatoes and tomatoes*). If the *o* is preceded by a vowel (*ratio, studio*), make it plural the conventional way, just by adding *s* (*ratios, studios*).

For numbers and letters, form the plural by adding *'s* (*the 1980's, M's and W's*).

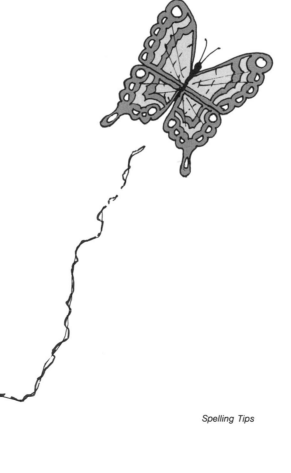

Hyphenate prefixes?

Generally, no. The only common prefixes that should regularly be separated from the main word by a hyphen are *ex* (*ex-president, ex-champion*) and *self* (*self-conscious, self-inflicted*). For most other common prefixes, no hyphen: (*bimonthly, counterproductive, interoffice, nonsexist, overpaid, redeposit, semiannual, untested*).

There are a few exceptions, but they're based on common sense: Do use a hyphen if the word following the prefix begins with a capital letter (*non-American, pre-Kennedy*); or if the last letter of the prefix is the same as the first letter of the word following (*anti-inflation, micro-organism*); or if the absence of a hyphen would probably invite mispronunciation (*co-op, mid-ear*).

Proofreading Symbols

SYMBOL	DESCRIPTION	STANDS FOR
☌	Pigtail stemming from crossed-out passage.	Delete.
⊗	X in a circle.	Period.
☰	Three short lines under a small letter.	Capital letter.
/	Diagonal line through a capital letter.	Small letter.
∽	Opposite-facing loops drawn around groups of words or letters.	Transpose.
⁋	Backwards P with a double stem.	New paragraph.
λ	Caret between words or letters, with line running out to margin.	Insert.
Stet	Applied to edited passage.	Let it stand.

EXAMPLE:

This . . .

In order to keep their editing/writing clear, professional writers use proofreading symbols. Although there are many more of these symbols most of the others/rest are only useful in the Publishing industry.

. . . means this

To keep their writing clear, professional writers use proofreading symbols.

There are many more of these symbols. Most of the rest are useful only in the publishing industry.

You and they or They and you?

They and you is correct. Here's why:

Many grammatical conventions develop out of concern for courtesy to others. Thus, in language usage, we normally put others ahead of ourselves (*You and I . . .* , NEVER *I and you . . .*). Likewise, we put people who aren't present (*He, She,* or *They*) ahead of those who are (*You* or *I*).

Stating it grammatically: Second person (*You*) should go ahead of first (*I, we*); and third (*He, She, They*) should go ahead of second (*You*). This is true whether the words are subjects, as in the preceding examples, or objects (*. . . you and me, . . . them and you*).

116

Glossary of
Grammar
Terms

Glossary of Grammar Terms

Accusative. Synonym for 'objective.' (See "Case.")

Active Voice. The verb form in which the subject performs the action rather than receiving it. (See "Parts of Speech: Verb: Voice.")

Antecedent. The word, usually a noun, that a pronoun stands for. It may also be a phrase or clause. (See "Parts of Speech: Pronoun.")

Article. There are only three articles in English: *a* and *an* (indefinite articles), and *the* (definite article). Because they modify nouns, they are adjectives.

Auxiliary Verb. (Also called 'helping verb.') Some form of the verb *to be* in front of another verb. The main verb may take several auxiliaries (The sale *should have been* completed by now).

Case. The form of a pronoun that tells whether it's used in a sentence as the subject (nominative), an object (objective, sometimes called 'accusative'), or possessor (possessive, sometimes called 'genitive'). Nouns in English change form only for the possessive (by adding *'s*).

Clause. A group of words that has a subject and predicate (verb). It may be a whole sentence or part of a sentence. There are two kinds: (1) **Independent C** can stand alone and be a complete sentence without the help of another clause (*All employees received raises*). (2) **Dependent C** (often called 'subordinate') qualifies or enlarges the idea of an independent clause and depends on it for meaning (*Although less than half belong to the union*).

Dependent clauses are further divided into two kinds: (a) **Nonrestrictive C** does not change the meaning of the main clause (The red brick building, *which contains the nuclear reactor*, is closed to the public). Nonrestrictive clauses are set off by commas. (b) **Restrictive C** changes or qualifies the meaning of the main clause (The red brick building *that contains the nuclear reactor* is closed to the public.) Restrictive clauses are not set off by commas.

You really must know how to recognize these if you are to use punctuation correctly.

Cliché. A group of words used as a common expression. Writers like to use them because clichés are usually colorful or impressive. But they are generally considered undesirable in serious writing; their meaning is often imprecise, and they are overused and become trite. They are never necessary.

Colloquial. Common, informal language. It carries neither the heaviness of formal vocabulary nor the undignified tone of slang. It is between the two and is probably the best kind of language for most writing and for all speeches. (This book is written in colloquial English.)

Complement. A word or phrase that completes (complements) the main verb of a sentence. It is part of the predicate and usually appears after the main verb (DeTocqueville, a French nobleman, wrote *an amazingly accurate study of American democracy*). In this case, *study* is the direct object of the transitive verb *wrote*. (See "Predicate.")

Complex Sentence. A sentence containing one independent clause and one or more dependent (subordinate) clauses. (See "Clause.")

Adjective

Adverb

See
page 27

118

Compound Sentence. One containing two or more independent clauses. Because they're independent, they must be joined by a comma and a coordinate conjunction (and, but, or, nor, for, yet). (See "Clause.")

Compound-Complex Sentence. Just as its name implies, it contains both the kinds described above. It contains two or more independent clauses (making it compound), and one of them has a dependent clause (making it complex).

Conjugation. The changing forms of a verb to show its function (number, person, tense, voice, and mood) in a given sentence. (See "Verb.")

Conjunctive Adverb. (*However, therefore, nevertheless, for example*, etc.) These connect independent clauses; therefore, they serve as conjunctions. But they modify the verb in the clause; therefore, they are technically adverbs. Like conjunctions, they're important to writing because they connect ideas—they help the reader **see** some logical relationship between clauses—a relationship the writer can **feel**—such as cause and effect (I think; *therefore*, I am). Unlike conjunctions, *however*, they can appear either at the beginning of the clause (as in the last sentence) or in the middle, close to the verb (as in this one). That choice gives writers choices of rhythm, variety, and emphasis. (See "Conjunction.")

Conjunction

See
page 27

Coordinate Clauses. The two independent clauses of a compound sentence, joined by a comma and a coordinate conjunction (and, but, or, nor, for, yet).

Dangling Modifier. A word or phrase that does not properly modify the part of the sentence the writer intended. Most common is: **Dangling Participle:** *Being the senior member present, the control panel was operated by Snavely.* (Strange control panel!)

Declension. The changing forms of a noun, pronoun, or adjective, in many languages, to show its exact function (number, sex, and case) in a given sentence. English has no noun or adjective declensions; a noun's function is shown by its position, and adjectives don't change. (See "Noun," "Adjective," and "Pronoun.")

Definite Article. *The* is the only definite article in English. So called because it specifies a particular thing (*the* quarterback), as opposed to **Indefinite** article, which does not specify a particular thing (*a* quarterback).

Dependent Clause. One not capable of standing alone as a sentence (*When you finish the report,*); it depends on an independent clause. (See "Clause.")

Direct Object. The noun or pronoun that receives the action of a transitive verb: (Our secretary [subject] answered [transitive verb] *the phone* [direct object]). It may also be a phrase or clause acting as a noun: (We [subject] are trying [transitive verb] *to find a solution to this problem* [direct object]).

Gender. The form of a pronoun that tells the sex of the noun (person) that pronoun stands for (he, she, it). Nouns also have gender in many languages, but in English almost all nouns are neuter. (Exceptions: actor-actress, widow-widower, etc.) Adjectives, too, have gender in many languages, but not in English. In French, for example, you can't simply describe something as *big*. It's *grand* if the thing you're describing is masculine (the table) and *grande* if it is feminine (the house). How do you know whether a noun is masculine or feminine? French infants have no trouble learning. But English-speaking people, used to simpler patterns, have fits memorizing these things when learning Romance languages as adults.

Genitive. Synonym for 'possessive.' (See "Case.")

Gerund. A verb used as a noun, always ending with *-ing*. It may be a subject (*Swimming* is the best of exercises) or an object (We attended the *opening*). Verb phrases, too, can be gerunds (People learn better by *seeing and hearing* than by either one alone).

Helping Verb. Another term for 'auxiliary verb.'

Idiom. A commonly accepted term that does not follow the rules of the language—in fact may even violate them (Passenger trains have *all but* vanished from American society). Idioms occur in all languages and are a curse to people learning a new language. We say "*Hurry up*," but "*Slow down*." Who can tell why? Although the literal meanings of *up* and *down* are opposites, their idiomatic meanings here are almost identical; yet, we dare not switch them. In English, prepositions are most often used idiomatically, and they cause fits to people learning English as a second language. No logic can explain why we say: Agreed *on*, hurry *up*, going *over*, chasing *after*, or *down* to the corner. (Also see "Colloquial" and "Slang.")

Imperative. The form (mood) of a verb that denotes command: "*Be* here promptly at ten." The subject (you) is omitted, implied. (See "Verb: Mood.")

Indefinite Article. *A* and *an* are the only indefinite articles in English. So called because they do not specify a particular thing (*a* computer program), as opposed to **Definite** article, which does specify a particular thing (*the* computer program).

Independent Clause. One capable of standing alone as a sentence without the help of any other words. Every sentence must have one. (See "Clause.")

Indicative. The most common form (mood) of verbs, denoting that the action is fact (All men *are created* equal). (See "Verb: Mood.")

Indirect Object. A second object of some transitive verbs, other than the direct object. It usually denotes the person or thing indirectly affected by the action of that verb (We [subject] sent [transitive verb] *him* [indirect object] flowers [direct object].) Note that the prepositon *to* is implied; the indirect object here is actually the object of the preposition.

Infinitive. The "to be" form of any verb (*to audit, to travel*, etc.). This is the basic verb form.

Interjection

See
page 27

Intransitive Verb. One that does not need an object to complete its meaning (My back *ached*). All passive voice verbs are intransitive (The instructions *were ignored*); the subject is the word that would be the direct object of a transitive verb if the same statement were in the active voice. Note, however, that not all intransitive verbs are passive voice. (See "Verb" and "Passive Voice.")

Jargon. The specialized language of a particular profession. It is a kind of short-hand, sometimes expressing complex ideas in a few words. But it is generally considered undesirable because only people in that profession can understand it. And it often complicates writing unnecessarily. Avoid it if possible.

Linking Verb. Every sentence must have a verb to give its subject a predicate. Usually the verb is active (the action is done by the subject to the object) or passive (the action is received by [done to] the subject). But occasionally it's neither, just *linking* the subject to something else. That something else is either a predicate adjective (Caviar *is* expensive) or predicate nominative (Caviar *is* fish eggs). Another name for linking verbs is 'copulative.'

Metaphor. A group of words that implies a comparison to something else, usually to create a vivid or colorful image (*Smedley is a tiger at the bridge table*). Though colorful, metaphors are generally imprecise, leaving the reader to decide exactly what the writer means. Different from simile, in which the comparison is direct. (See "Simile.")

Mixed Metaphor. Two metaphors that contradict each other or for some other reason are not appropriate when used together (*She climbed the ladder of success with both feet planted firmly on the ground*). The writer guilty of such thoughtless expression invites ridicule—and deserves it.

Modify. To describe further the meaning of another word. (In the statement just finished, *further* modifies *describe*.) In English, adjectives modify nouns (*modern* office) or pronouns; adverbs modify verbs (*strongly* objected), adjectives, or other adverbs. The modifier, and that which it modifies, may be a clause or phrase rather than an individual word.

Mood. The form of a verb that tells whether the action it describes is fact (indicative mood), command (imperative mood), or condition contrary to fact (subjunctive mood). (See "Verb.")

Nominative. The form (case) of a pronoun that denotes it is the subject of its sentence (*We* [subject] demanded [transitive verb] a refund [direct object].) (See "Case" and "Pronouns.")

Nonrestrictive Clause. A dependent (subordinate) clause that adds to but does not limit the meaning of the main clause to which it is attached. It is separated from the main clause by commas (The increase in crime, *which is everybody's concern*, has many causes). A good test: If you can remove it without causing the meaning of the remaining part to be inaccurate, it's nonrestrictive. (See "Clause.")

Object. The noun or pronoun that receives the action of a verb, or that is linked to a preposition. (It may also be a noun phrase or clause.) (See "Direct Object," "Indirect Object," "Intransitive Verb," and "Transitive Verb.")

Objective. The form (case) of a pronoun that denotes it is an object in its sentence: "They (subject) asked *me* (indirect object) to mail *it* (direct object) to *them* (object of preposition)." Also called 'accusative.' (See "Case," "Object," and "Pronouns.")

Participle. A word derived from a verb but used as an adjective (so named because it *participates* as both). Commonly used as a simple adjective (The *nominating* committee; the *retired* executive).

Also, the latter part of a verb, following some form of *to be*. A few of the possible forms: (He is *asking* [present participle, active voice]); (He has *asked* [past participle, active voice]); (He had *asked* [past perfect participle, active voice]); (He will *ask* [future participle, active voice]); (He will have been *asked* [future perfect participle, passive voice]). All of these participles are technically adjectives, because they modify the subject of the 'to be' part of the verb. (See "Adjective," "Verb," and "Dangling Modifier.")

Passive Voice. The intransitive verb form in which the subject receives the action of the verb rather than performing the action. In passive constructions, the object (of a preposition) performs the action (The battalion *was inspected* by the base commander). Or, there may be no object and hence no stated source of the action (The battalion *was inspected*). (See "Adjective," "Verb," and "Dangling Modifier.")

Noun

See
page 27

Perfect. The verb form which denotes that the action reported by the verb was complete at the time being reported: "She *had finished* her speech before I arrived." (See "Participle.")

Phrase. A group of words lacking a subject or a verb, or both, but serving as some part of speech in a sentence. (Distinguished from a *clause*, which must have a subject and a verb.) Phrases may serve as a noun (*Giving to charity* is a solemn obligation), adjective (*Higher-than-average* earnings), verb (The lab *has been working* on this all year), or adverb (We failed, *like those before us*). Note that the noun phrase above is a gerund (verb serving as a subject). Most common are prepositional phrases. (*At each location; Before buying*); these, however, always serve in sentences as adjectives or adverbs. Many prepositional phrases are badly overused in business writing and are often called "rubber stamp phrases" (*prior to, in accordance with, in response to*). Phrases may be nonrestrictive or restrictive.

As with clauses, you really must know how to recognize and understand phrases if you are to use punctuation correctly.

Possessive. The form (case) of a noun or pronoun that denotes ownership. In English, nouns are made possessive simply by adding *'s*. Pronouns change form entirely: (*I* felt as though *my* [possessive-nominative] body were not really *mine* [possessive-objective]). Also called 'genitive.' (See "Case" and "Pronouns.")

Predicate. The part of a sentence or clause containing the main verb, which makes some statement about its subject (The hovercraft ride from Dover to Calais *was the most interesting part of the trip*. René Descartes, a French philosopher, *made the simple but profound statement, "I think; therefore, I am."*)

Predicate Adjective. An adjective used to complete a linking verb. This is grammar at its trickiest. (Rush hour traffic is *heavy*.) Although *heavy* is part of the sentence's predicate, or verb statement, it's an adjective modifying the noun *traffic*. You could probably live 100 years and not know this, yet still use grammar correctly.

Predicate Nominative. Like a predicate adjective, it's used to complete a linking verb. (She is the *chairwoman*.) Although *chairwoman* is part of the predicate, or verb statement, it's a noun (hence 'nominative') modifying the pronoun *she*. This is pretty heady stuff. But if you're going to boast to friends about predicate adjectives, you probably ought to know this too.

Preposition

Pronoun

See
page 27

Restrictive Clause. A dependent (subordinate) clause that limits the meaning of the main clause. It is not set off by commas (All employees *who have been with the company ten years or longer* were invited to the dinner). A good test: If you cannot remove it without causing the meaning of the remaining part to be inaccurate, it's restrictive. (See "Clause.")

Sentence. A group of words expressing a complete thought. It must contain at least one independent clause, and it must begin with a capital letter and end with a period (or other ending punctuation). It contains a subject (usually a noun or pronoun) and a predicate (some statement about that subject, containing the verb). All the rules of grammar, including punctuation, serve one purpose: to help writers construct *individual sentences*, one at a time, that are clear to the reader. (See "Simple Sentence," "Compound Sentence," "Complex Sentence," and "Compound-Complex Sentence.")

Sentence Fragment. A part of a sentence standing as a sentence (as here). Even the strictest grammarians approve the use of an occasional sentence fragment. Two rules should limit their use, however: (1) Keep them short, so the reader can tell that the omission is deliberate rather than the result of carelessness. (2) Use them only occasionally; the reader feels uncomfortable if you break conventional patterns very often.

Simile. A group of words that makes a direct comparison to something else, usually to create an image (You behaved *like a child*; The rear engine of the DC-10 is *as large as the entire fusilage of the old DC-3*). Different from a metaphor, in which the comparison is indirect. (See "Metaphor.")

Simple Sentence. A sentence containing one independent clause and no dependent clauses (*They completed the test*). In spite of its title, a simple sentence may be complicated. It may contain phrases, compound subject or verb, and several modifiers (*We and the government representatives must work together and respect the needs of our schools and colleges in this most difficult of projects*).

Slang. Informal language, usually considered undignified except in writing to close friends or loved ones. (Differs from *colloquial*, which is informal but dignified enough for all but the most formal writing.) In English, slang often gains dignity gradually through common usage and becomes colloquial. Slang is also considered less dignified than *idiom*, which is commonly accepted language that does not follow rules or literal definitions. (See "Colloquial" and "Idiom.")

Subject. The part of a sentence or clause that connects with the main verb (predicate), by either performing or receiving the action of that verb. The subject names the person, place, or thing about which that sentence makes a statement. It is usually a noun or pronoun. But it may also be a gerund (*Walking* is good exercise), a phrase (*To succeed in business* is not every person's goal), or a clause (*Whoever makes the sale* should supervise the delivery).

Subjunctive. The form (mood) of a verb which denotes that the action or condition described by that verb is contrary to fact (If I *were* president). (See "Verb: Mood.")

Subordinate Clause. Another name for dependent clause. So called because the information it contains is less important than (subordinate to) that in the main clause on which it depends.

Syntax. Sentence structure; the order or relationship of the words in a sentence.

Tense. The form of a verb that denotes whether the action it describes is in the past, present, or future. (See "Verb" and "Participle.")

Transitive Verb. One that needs an object (direct object) to complete its meaning. In English, by far the most commonly used sentence structure is: subject, transitive verb, direct object: *A rolling stone* (subject) *gathers* (transitive verb) *no moss* (direct object). There can be no sensible meaning to *A rolling stone gathers*.

Verbal. A word formed from a verb but used as something else. The three common types are gerunds, infinitives, and participles.

Voice. The form of a verb that tells whether the subject performs the action that verb describes (active voice), or receives it (passive voice). (See "Verb," "Active," and "Passive.")

Verb

See page 28

Post-course Test

1. **What part of speech is the italicized word?**
   The beleaguered nation wants $61 million of foreign aid in the current fiscal *year*.

   _____.

2. **Should the two parts of the sentence below be separated by a comma?**
   Smedley called to confirm the order / and asked that you return the call.
   _____ yes   _____ no

3. **Is the italicized passage a phrase or a clause?**
   Few people know *that Ian Fleming, author of the James Bond spy novels, also wrote children's stories*. _____ phrase   _____ clause

4. **Does the italicized pronoun match its noun (antecedent)?**
   You may have an employee who has seen changes year in and year out, and *they* should be on the planning committee. _____ yes   _____ no

5. **True or false:**
   A good rule in building sentences is: Try not to put much other information between a subject and its verb. _____ true   _____ false

6. **Is the italicized phrase restrictive or nonrestrictive?**
   Christopher Columbus is buried *in the Dominican Republic*.
   _____ restrictive   _____ nonrestrictive

7. **What part of speech is the italicized word?**
   The prosecutor criticized school officials for their handling of *athletic* scholarships.

   _____.

8. **True or false:**
   You can avoid passive voice verbs by keeping the action in the present or future tense.
   _____ true   _____ false

9. **What part of speech is the italicized word?**
   Certainly I like artichokes, but I wouldn't say I love *them*.

   _____.

10. **Are the italicized pronouns used correctly?**
    That decision is for *he and I* to make. _____ yes   _____ no

11. **True or false:**
    A paragraph is a group of related sentences; therefore, it's improper to write a one-sentence paragraph. _____ true   _____ false

12. **Which is better writing style?**
    _____ The compressor needs to be oiled regularly. In all such units, proper lubrication is vital.

    _____ The compressor needs to be oiled regularly. In all such compressors, proper lubrication is vital.

13. **Is the italicized clause dependent or independent?**
    Politicians who speak at universities and professional meetings *often get $5,000 for an hour or less*. _____ dependent   _____ independent

14. **What part of speech is the italicized word?**

    The Clippers were an *extremely* lucky team last year. _____.

15. **Is the italicized passage a phrase or a clause?**
    The hunchback of Notre Dame is a famous heroic character in French literature.
    _____ phrase _____ clause

16. **True or false:**
    Who's who should be worded *who's whom.* _____ true _____ false

17. **Is the italicized word a subject, transitive verb, or direct object?**
    The Beatles performed their first U.S. *concert* in Carnegie Hall.
    _____ subject _____ transitive verb _____ direct object

18. **Should the two parts of the sentence below be separated by a comma?**
    Tomorrow is my birthday / and I'm taking the day off. _____ yes _____ no

19. **What part of speech is the italicized phrase?**
    Be sure to send Cookie's new impressions *to the veterinary lab*.

    _____.

20. **Tell what's wrong with the sentence below, and correct it.**
    Smith was found guilty, but instead of going to jail the judge put her on probation.

    The error is called: _____.

    Corrected: _____

    _____.

21. **Should there be a comma at the slash (/) mark?**
    George Brett, like other great baseball players / trying for a hitting record, felt that the
    pressure of public opinion hurt him. _____ yes _____ no

22. **Does the italicized pronoun match its noun (antecedent)?**
    Our experts know where you can cut your food costs, and we'd like to share *it* with you.
    _____ yes _____ no

23. **Tell what's wrong with the sentence below, and correct it.**
    You must define the objective this particular group of people want to achieve.

    The error is: _____.

    Corrected: _____

    _____.

24. **Is the italicized passage a phrase or a clause?**
    Benjamin Franklin invented many things *but is not recognized as a great inventor or
    scientist.* _____ phrase _____ clause

25. **What part of speech is the italicized word?**
    American Indians introduced popcorn *to* the colonists on February 22, 1630.

    _____.

*Post-course
Test:*
*Things you
MUST know*

*(Answer Key:
pages 139
through 146)*

26. **What part of speech is the italicized clause?**

    I don't know *what you should do.* _____.

27. **Is the italicized clause restrictive or nonrestrictive?**
    People *who play the flute* are called flautists. _____ restrictive _____ nonrestrictive

28. **What part of speech is the italicized word?**

    The hand *that* rocks the cradle rocks the world. _____.

29. **Is the italicized clause dependent or independent?**
    I acted surprised *because I thought you were out of town.*
    _____ dependent _____ independent

30. **True or false:**
    The shorter a sentence is, the harder it hits. _____ true _____ false

31. **Is the italicized word a subject, transitive verb, or direct object?**
    George Washington *placed* the first stone of the U.S. Capitol building.
    _____ subject _____ transitive verb _____ direct object

32. **True or false:**
    Thoughtful writers sometimes begin sentences with *and* or *but,* so they can have both the smooth flow of connectives and the impact of short sentences. There has never been a rule against doing this. _____ true _____ false

33. **What part of speech is the italicized word?**
    The number of children dying of cancer has dropped *sharply* in the last three decades.

    _____.

34. **Should the two parts of the sentence below be separated by a comma?**
    In 1983 / the Cavaliers may have been the worst team in professional sports.
    _____ yes _____ no

35. **What part of speech is the italicized phrase?**

    A well-dressed woman should not wear a watch *at night.* _____.

36. **What part of speech is the italicized phrase?**

    Yak's milk is pink. _____.

37. **What part of speech is the italicized clause?**
    Computers *that correct grammar* haven't been very successful.

    _____.

38. **What part of speech are the italicized words?**

    Acid rain *is damaging* India's famous Taj Mahal. _____.

39. **True or false:**
    A phrase always serves as one of the parts of speech. _____ true _____ false

40. **Should there be a comma at the slash (/) mark?**
    The American Goldfinch, unlike most other birds / lays eggs and has chicks in late summer. _____ yes _____ no

41. **Does the italicized pronoun match its noun (antecedent)?**
    You'll never find a tiger in Africa; *they're* found only in Asia. _____ yes _____ no

42. **What part of speech is the italicized word?**

    You are the only person here who can speak Spanish. _____.

43. **Tell what's wrong with the sentence below, and correct it.**
    Each of the new employees require special training.

    The error is: _____.

    Corrected: _____

    _____.

44. **What part of speech is the italicized word?**
    Hotels *and* restaurants are more expensive in Singapore than in Hong Kong.

    _____.

45. **What part of speech is the italicized clause?**
    Anyone *who wants the increased hospitalization benefits* should fill out the attached form.

    _____.

46. **What part of speech is the italicized word?**

    Look, this doesn't make sense at all. _____   _____.

47. **What part of speech is the italicized clause?**
    When you're Smedley's bridge partner, you'd better have a good sense of humor.

    _____.

48. **Is the italicized phrase restrictive or nonrestrictive?**
    Qantas, *the name of the Australian airline,* stands for Queensland and Northern Territories
    Air Service. _____ restrictive _____ nonrestrictive

49. **What part of speech is the italicized word?**

    This is the *last* one. _____   _____.

50. **Is the italicized clause dependent or independent?**
    I'm tired, *and I'm going home.* _____ dependent _____ independent

51. **True or false:**
    To turn passive voice verbs active, ask yourself "by whom"; the answer to that question
    should be the subject. _____ true _____ false

52. **True or false:**
    You can justify using plural pronouns with singular subjects to avoid sexist references
    such as *he.* _____ true _____ false

53. **Is the italicized passage a phrase or a clause?**
    It's ironic that Alfred Nobel, *who invented dynamite,* also established the Peace Prize.
    _____ phrase _____ clause

54. **Is the italicized word a subject, transitive verb, or direct object?**
    Eight *reindeer* pull Santa's sleigh.
    _____ subject _____ transitive verb _____ direct object

Post-course Test:

Things you MUST know

(Answer Key: pages 139 through 146)

55. **True or false:**
Thoughtful writers *do* repeat key words rather than seeking synonyms.
_____ true _____ false

56. **What part of speech is the italicized word?**
The exact delivery date is not certain, *but* we think it will be in two or three weeks.

_____.

57. **Is the italicized pronoun used correctly?**
Pollsters are trying to find out *who* New York voters are supporting.
_____ yes _____ no

58. **True or false:**
A clause can always stand alone and make sense. _____ true _____ false

59. **Should the two parts of the sentence below be separated by a comma?**
Theodore Roosevelt wrote 37 books / but few of them are well known.
_____ yes _____ no

60. **What part of speech is the italicized word?**

What do the letters S.P.C.A. stand *for*? _____.

61. **Should the two parts of the sentence below be separated by a comma?**
We questioned as many employees as we could / and learned that most union members are for the change. _____ yes _____ no

62. **What part of speech is the italicized clause?**
When the lava came within a mile of the village, the inhabitants were evacuated.

_____.

63. **What part of speech are the italicized words?**
The ground ball that drove in the winning run *was ruled* an error.

_____.

64. **Should there be a comma at the slash (/) mark?**
Smedley, who won first prize last year / is doing even better so far this year.
_____ yes _____ no

65. **Tell what's wrong with the sentence below, and correct it.**
A minimum of 10 qualifying segments are needed to obtain a free flight certificate.

The error is: _____.

Corrected: _____

_____.

66. **What part of speech is the italicized word?**
Cappelletti emphasized that the city *wants* the work to continue.

_____.

67. **Is the italicized clause restrictive or nonrestrictive?**
Crocuses, *although they often bloom before winter ends,* are not affected by cold or snow. _____ restrictive _____ nonrestrictive

68. **What part of speech is the italicized clause?**

What goes up must come down. _____.

69. **True or false:**
Passive voice verbs hinder readers by tempting writers to leave out the words that tell who does what. _____ true _____ false

70. **Which is better writing style?**
_____ The branch chief liked the idea. Harry, who was worried about schedules, loved it.

_____ The branch chief liked the idea. And Harry, who was worried about schedules, loved it.

_____ The branch chief liked the idea, and Harry, who was worried about schedules, loved it.

71. **Is the italicized clause restrictive or nonrestrictive?**
The only machine *that can do this job* is made in Canada.
_____ restrictive _____ nonrestrictive

72. **True or false:**
The easiest way to avoid sexism in your writing is to switch to the plural.
_____ true _____ false

73. **What part of speech is the italicized word?**
Political *observers* believe she would be hard put to win any delegates.

_____.

74. **Which is better writing style?**
_____ White paint reflects sunlight and also makes most structures seem larger.

_____ White paint, which also makes most structures seem larger, reflects sunlight.

75. **Is the italicized passage a phrase or a clause?**
Ontario is the only Canadian province *that borders the Great Lakes*.
_____ phrase _____ clause

76. **Is the italicized word a subject, transitive verb, or direct object?**
African elephants have larger *ears* than Indian elephants.
_____ subject _____ transitive verb _____ direct object

77. **What part of speech is the italicized word?**

Oh, what a beautiful morning! _____.

78. **Tell what's wrong with the sentence below, and correct it.**
After Tommy's successful surgery, Action 4 newscaster Mickey Burrell says he just wants to go home and get some rest.

The error is called: _____.

Corrected: _____

_____.

79. **Is the italicized verb transitive or intransitive?**
Insects *are* the oldest class of animals. _____ transitive _____ intransitive

80. **Should the two parts of the sentence below be separated by a comma?**
Oliver Wendell Holmes was a famous Supreme Court Justice / but was never Chief Justice. _____ yes _____ no

81. **Should the two parts of the sentence below be separated by a comma?**
In the seven races of the 1983 Americas Cup Competition / the Australians used an unconventional design and beat the Americans for the first time in a century.
_____ yes _____ no

82. **What part of speech is the italicized phrase?**
People *under six feet tall* shouldn't seek careers as basketball players.

_____.

83. **What part of speech is the italicized phrase?**
Octopuses, *considered by many to be monsters of the deep,* are actually small and harmless.

_____.

84. **Should the two parts of the sentence below be separated by a comma?**
When you left town / things just weren't the same. _____ yes _____ no

85. **Tell what's wrong with the sentence below, and correct it.**
After spending 20 minutes in the icy water, rescuers finally arrived and pulled the child to safety.

The error is called: _____.

Corrected: _____

_____.

86. **Should the two parts of the sentence below be separated by a comma?**
I would like to thank you for your support / which has been very helpful.
_____ yes _____ no

87. **What part of speech is the italicized phrase?**
In accordance with the specifications of your March 16 letter relative to federal regulations governing the import and export of spider eggs, Form 1E 2619-4437-DD-2 is enclosed.

_____.

88. **Should there be a comma at the slash (/) mark?**
The more time zones you cross, and the faster you cross them / the more severe your jet lag is likely to be. _____ yes _____ no

89. **What part of speech is the italicized word?**
Ask your *department* head for the hospitalization forms. _____.

90. **Is the italicized pronoun used correctly?**
The ideal arrangement would be for Bradley Corp. and *us* to share the work.
_____ yes _____ no

1. **Should the comma be in the sentence below?**
   I ordered fried shrimp, but the waiter brought linguini with clam sauce.
   _____ yes   _____ no

2. **What punctuation mark will most effectively separate the parts of the sentence below?**
   Research scientists don't like to report details of projects that fail __?__ you can understand why.

   _____.

3. **Which of these is correctly punctuated?**
   _____ Tomorrow we're leaving for London.

   _____ Tomorrow, we're leaving for London.

   _____ Both are correct.

4. **Which of these is correctly punctuated?**
   _____ The day after the project is completed and approved by the staff we're leaving for London.
   _____ The day after the project is completed and approved by the staff, we're leaving for London.

5. **Which is correct?**
   _____ The Catawba vines were the only ones which survived.

   _____ The Catawba vines were the only ones that survived.

6. **Which of these is correctly punctuated?**
   _____ "We were directly involved," the young producer said, "and it was beautiful."

   _____ "We were directly involved", the young producer said, "and it was beautiful".

7. **Is the sentence below punctuated correctly?**
   The 51 professionals, representing 40 alcoholism and drug treatment agencies were unanimous that the state isn't doing enough. _____ yes   _____ no

8. **Tell what's wrong with the sentence below, and improve it.**
   The problems of the Middle East are not without solutions if all involved really want solutions.

   The trouble is: _____.

   Improved: _____

   _____

9. **What punctuation mark is needed between the two parts of the sentence below?**
   One point should be obvious to everyone __?__ this machine can't do the job much longer.

   _____   _____.

10. **What punctuation mark will best separate the two parts of the sentence below?**

    Frogs have teeth __?__ toads do not. _____.

Post-course Test:

Things you SHOULD know

(Answer Key: pages 147 through 151)

11. **Should the comma be in the sentence below?**
The rain continued all day, and turned to snow just before rush hour.
_____ yes _____ no

12. **Which of these is correct?**
_____ None of these has been inspected.

_____ None of these have been inspected.

13. **True or false:**
Syntax is the art of building words into effective sentences. _____ true _____ false

14. **Which of these is correct?**
_____ Several of your findings are different from ours.

_____ Several of your findings are different than ours.

15. **Which of these is correctly punctuated?**
_____ Wallpaper, carpeting and drapes have not been installed yet.

_____ Wallpaper, carpeting, and drapes have not been installed yet.

16. **Tell what's wrong with the sentence below, and correct it.**
Bianca can play flute, piano, guitar, and sing second soprano.

The error is called: _____.

Corrected: _____

_____.

17. **Which of these is correctly punctuated?**
_____ One of the contestants is my brother; therefore I shouldn't be a judge.

_____ One of the contestants is my brother; therefore, I shouldn't be a judge.

18. **What is the structure of the sentence below?**
Anyone who can't swim should learn how.
_____ simple _____ compound _____ complex

19. **Which of these is correct?**
_____ The 16-bit system, which uses interactive software programs, allows us to add terminals later.

_____ The 16-bit system, that uses interactive software programs, allows us to add terminals later.

20. **What punctuation marks will most effectively separate the parts of the sentence below?**
If you want to improve your computer skills __?__ and I know you do __?__ you should attend this seminar.

_____.

21. **What punctuation mark is needed between the two parts of the sentence below?**
Franklin D. Roosevelt was president of the U.S. longer than any other person __?__ he served 3-1/2 terms, for 13 years.

_____.

22. **What is the structure of the sentence below?**
I'm tired, and I'm hungry.
_____ compound _____ complex _____ compound/complex

23. **What punctuation mark will best separate the two parts of the sentence below?**
Chief Justice Warren Burger is critical of American lawyers __?__ he thinks they lack civility.

_____.

24. **Tell what's wrong with the sentence below, and improve it.**
It would not have been surprising if Yarborough had not done well that day.

The trouble is: _____.

Improved: _____

_____.

25. **What punctuation mark is needed between the two parts of the sentence below?**
Only one National Football League team does not have decorations on the sides of its helmets __?__ the Cleveland Browns.

_____.

26. **Which of these is correct?**
_____ The central processing unit has 2 disk drives.

_____ The central processing unit has two disk drives.

27. **Should the comma be in the sentence below?**
The hospital is overcrowded, and patient care has suffered as a result.
_____ yes _____ no

28. **Which of these is correct?**
_____ The system now has 27 terminals.

_____ The system now has twenty-seven terminals.

29. **Tell what's wrong with the sentence below, and correct it.**
We can only assure you that these changes were observed regularly in the findings.

The trouble is: _____ _____.

Corrected: _____

_____.

30. **True or false:**
Use *that* for restrictive clauses and *which* for nonrestrictive. _____ true _____ false

31. **What punctuation mark is needed between the two parts of the sentence below?**
Albert Blake Dick invented the mimeograph machine __?__ and the A. B. Dick Co. is named after him.

_____.

Post-course
Test:

Things you
SHOULD know

(Answer Key:
pages 147
through 151)

32. **What is the structure of the sentence in Question 31?**

_____ simple _____ compound _____ complex

33. **Tell what's wrong with the sentence below, and correct it.**

Certificates will only be issued to registered contestants.

The trouble is: _____.

Corrected: _____.

34. **Correct the sentence below.**
Hopefully, you'll be able to join me this week-end. _____

_____

35. **True or false:**
A prepositional phrase always serves as an adjective or an adverb.
_____ true _____ false

36. **What punctuation would be most effective between the two parts of the sentence below?**
California does not have the longest coastline of any U.S. state __?__ Alaska has.

_____.

37. **Tell what's wrong with the sentence below, and correct it.**
A well-dressed woman only wears diamonds at night.

The error is called: _____.

Corrected: _____

_____

38. **What punctuation mark would be most effective between the two parts of the sentence below?**
Upward-curved corners on Chinese roofs serve an important purpose __?__ they keep evil spirits away.

_____.

39. **Tell what's wrong with the sentence below, and correct it.**
Once we were able to actually administer the venum, the child's condition began to quickly stabilize.

The errors are called: _____.

Corrected: _____

_____

40. **True or false:**
    Passive voice verbs are a bit dull because the subject receives the action rather than performing it. _____ true _____ false

41. **True or false:**
    A clause doesn't need a subject or a verb, but a phrase needs both.
    _____ true _____ false

42. **Should the comma be in the sentence below?**
    The maintenance representative still hasn't arrived, but has promised to be here first thing tomorrow morning. _____ yes _____ no

43. **Which of these is correct?**
    _____ Uniplan is hard disk system.

    _____ Uniplan is a hard-disk system.

44. **True or false:**
    Who's Who should be *Who's Whom.* _____ true _____ false

Post-course Test:

Things you SHOULD know

(Answer Key: pages 147 through 151)

1. **English is in the family of languages called:**
   _____ Romance   _____ Teutonic   _____ Anglo-Saxon

2. **The person who most affected the development of English is:**
   _____ Shakespeare   _____ King James   _____ William the Conqueror

3. **English grammar is in the category called:**
   _____ Syntactical   _____ Inflectional   _____ Transitive

4. **That means:**
   _____ Nouns and pronouns don't have gender (sex).
   _____ Every sentence must have a subject and verb.
   _____ The role of words is determined by their positions.

5. **True or false: English is known for the ease with which it accepts change.**
   _____ true   _____ false

6. **The most famous literary work from the Old English period is:**
   _____ The vulgate Bible   _____ Beowulf   _____ The Canterbury Tales

7. **Old English was a mixture of:**
   _____ Gaelic and Teutonic
   _____ Anglo-Saxon and Latin
   _____ Anglo-Saxon and French

8. **English grammar is known for its:**
   _____ Simplicity   _____ Complexity   _____ Poetic choices

9. **True or false:**
   English uses the Roman alphabet because it is best suited for a language of such diverse characteristics.
   _____ true   _____ false

10. **Middle English was a mixture of:**
    _____ Gaelic and Latin
    _____ Anglo-Saxon and French
    _____ Anglo-Saxon and Latin

11. **The works of Shakespeare are hard to understand today because:**
    _____ We are unaccustomed to the word order of sentences ending with verbs.
    _____ He wrote for the wealthy aristocrats of the London court.
    _____ English has changed so much since the Elizabethan Age.

12. **True or false:**
    What Americans think of as a British accent is a relatively new style of pronunciation. The pilgrims on the Mayflower spoke an English that sounded much like today's American English.
    _____ true   _____ false

1. **What part of speech is the italicized word?**
   The beleaguered nation wants $61 million of foreign aid in the current fiscal *year*.
   Noun (object of the preposition *in*). _____   Page 27.

2. **Should the two parts of the sentence below be separated by a comma?**
   Smedley called to confirm the order / and asked that you return the call.
   _____ yes ___✔___ no   Page 49.

Answer Key

to pages 126
through 132

*Things you
MUST know*

3. **Is the italicized passage a phrase or a clause?**
   Few people know *that Ian Fleming, author of the James Bond spy novels, also wrote children's stories*. _____ phrase ___✔___ clause   Page 38.

4. **Does the italicized pronoun match its noun (antecedent)?**
   You may have an employee who has seen changes year in and year out, and *they* should be on the planning committee. _____ yes ___✔___ no   Page 75.

5. **True or false:**
   A good rule in building sentences is: Try not to put much other information between a subject and its verb. ___✔___ true _____ false   Page 52.

6. **Is the italicized phrase restrictive or nonrestrictive?**
   Christopher Columbus is buried *in the Dominican Republic*.
   ___✔___ restrictive _____ nonrestrictive   Page 37.

7. **What part of speech is the italicized word?**
   The prosecutor criticized school officials for their handling of *athletic* scholarships.
   Adjective (modifies *scholarships*). _____   Page 27.

8. **True or false:**
   You can avoid passive voice verbs by keeping the action in the present or future tense.
   _____ true ___✔___ false   Page 91.

9. **What part of speech is the italicized word?**
   Certainly I like artichokes, but I wouldn't say I love *them*.
   Pronoun (direct object of *love*). _____   Page 27.

10. **Are the italicized pronouns used correctly?**
    That decision is for *he and I* to make. _____ yes ___✔___ no   Page 77.

11. **True or false:**
    A paragraph is a group of related sentences; therefore, it's improper to write a one-sentence paragraph. _____ true ___✔___ false   Page 99.

12. **Which is better writing style?**
    _____ The compressor needs to be oiled regularly. In all such units, proper lubrication is vital.

    ___✔___ The compressor needs to be oiled regularly. In all such compressors, proper lubrication is vital.   Page 98.

13. **Is the italicized clause dependent or independent?**
    Politicians who speak at universities and professional meetings *often get $5,000 for an hour or less*. _____ dependent ___✔___ independent   Page 38.

14. **What part of speech is the italicized word?**

The Clippers were an *extremely* lucky team last year. ___Adverb (modifies *lucky*).___

Page 38.

15. **Is the italicized passage a phrase or a clause?**
The hunchback of Notre Dame is a famous heroic character in French literature.
___✔___ phrase _____ clause   Page 37.

16. **True or false:**
Who's who should be worded *who's whom.* _____ true ___✔___ false   Page 77.

17. **Is the italicized word a subject, transitive verb, or direct object?**
The Beatles performed their first U.S. *concert* in Carnegie Hall.
_____ subject _____ transitive verb ___✔___ direct object   Page 48.

18. **Should the two parts of the sentence below be separated by a comma?**
Tomorrow is my birthday / and I'm taking the day off. ___✔___ yes _____ no
Page 49.

19. **What part of speech is the italicized phrase?**
Be sure to send Cookie's new impressions *to the veterinary lab.*
Adverb (modifies *send*). _____   Page 37.

20. **Tell what's wrong with the sentence below, and correct it.**
Smith was found guilty, but instead of going to jail the judge put her on probation.

The error is called: ___Dangling participle._____

Corrected: ___. . . instead of sending her to jail the judge . . . .___

_____(The judge didn't go to jail.)   Page 74.

21. **Should there be a comma at the slash (/) mark?**
George Brett, like other great baseball players / trying for a hitting record, felt that the pressure of public opinion hurt him. _____ yes ___✔___ no   Page 63.

22. **Does the italicized pronoun match its noun (antecedent)?**
Our experts know where you can cut your food costs, and we'd like to share *it* with you.
_____ yes ___✔___ no   Page 76.

23. **Tell what's wrong with the sentence below, and correct it.**
You must define the objective this particular group of people want to achieve.

The error is: ___Subject and verb don't agree._____

Corrected: ___. . . this group of people wants to achieve.___

_____(Singular subject [*group*] needs singular verb.)   Page 75.

24. **Is the italicized passage a phrase or a clause?**
Benjamin Franklin invented many things *but is not recognized as a great inventor or scientist.* ___✔___ phrase _____ clause   Page 37.

25. **What part of speech is the italicized word?**
American Indians introduced popcorn *to* the colonists on February 22, 1630.
Preposition. _____   Page 27.

26. **What part of speech is the italicized clause?**
I don't know *what you should do*. __Noun (direct object).__   Page 39.

27. **Is the italicized clause restrictive or nonrestrictive?**
People *who play the flute* are called flautists. __✔__ restrictive _____ nonrestrictive
Page 39.

28. **What part of speech is the italicized word?**
The hand *that* rocks the cradle rocks the world. __Pronoun.__   Page 27.

29. **Is the italicized clause dependent or independent?**
I acted surprised *because I thought you were out of town*.
__✔__ dependent _____ independent   Page 38.

30. **True or false:**
The shorter a sentence is, the harder it hits. __✔__ true _____ false   Page 51.

31. **Is the italicized word a subject, transitive verb, or direct object?**
George Washington *placed* the first stone of the U.S. Capitol building.
_____ subject __✔__ transitive verb _____ direct object   Page 48.

32. **True or false:**
Thoughtful writers sometimes begin sentences with *and* or *but,* so they can have both the smooth flow of connectives and the impact of short sentences. There has never been a rule against doing this. __✔__ true _____ false   Page 96.

33. **What part of speech is the italicized word?**
The number of children dying of cancer has dropped *sharply* in the last three decades.
Adverb (modifies *dropped*). _____   Page 27.

34. **Should the two parts of the sentence below be separated by a comma?**
In 1983 / the Cavaliers may have been the worst team in professional sports.
_____ yes _____ no __✔__ optional   Page 63.

35. **What part of speech is the italicized phrase?**
A well-dressed woman should not wear a watch *at night*. __Adverb.__   Page 37.

36. **What part of speech is the italicized phrase?**
Yak's milk is pink. __Noun (subject).__ _____   Page 37.

37. **What part of speech is the italicized clause?**
Computers *that correct grammar* haven't been very successful.
Adjective. _____   Page 39.

38. **What part of speech are the italicized words?**
Acid rain *is damaging* India's famous Taj Mahal. __Verb.__   Page 28.

39. **True or false:**
A phrase always serves as one of the parts of speech. ___✔___ true _____ false
Page 37.

40. **Should there be a comma at the slash (/) mark?**
The American Goldfinch, unlike most other birds / lays eggs and has chicks in late summer. ___✔___ yes _____ no
Page 37.

41. **Does the italicized pronoun match its noun (antecedent)?**
You'll never find a tiger in Africa; *they're* found only in Asia. _____ yes ___✔___ no
(No plural noun is nearby.)
Page 75.

42. **What part of speech is the italicized word?**
You are the only person here who can speak Spanish. __Pronoun.__
Page 27.

43. **Tell what's wrong with the sentence below, and correct it.**
Each of the new employees require special training.

The error is: ___Subject and verb don't agree.___

Corrected: ___Each of the new employees requires special training.___

_____ (Singular subject [*each*] needs singular verb.)
Page 75.

44. **What part of speech is the italicized word?**
Hotels *and* restaurants are more expensive in Singapore than in Hong Kong.
Conjunction
Page 27.

45. **What part of speech is the italicized clause?**
Anyone *who wants the increased hospitalization benefits* should fill out the attached form.
Adjective (modifies *anyone*).
Page 39.

46. **What part of speech is the italicized word?**
Look, this doesn't make sense at all. __Interjection.__
Page 27.

47. **What part of speech is the italicized clause?**
When you're Smedley's bridge partner, you'd better have a good sense of humor.
Adverb (modifies *have*).
Page 39.

48. **Is the italicized phrase restrictive or nonrestrictive?**
Qantas, *the name of the Australian airline,* stands for Queensland and Northern Territories Air Service. _____ restrictive ___✔___ nonrestrictive
Page 37.

49. **What part of speech is the italicized word?**
This is the *last* one. __Adjective (modifies *one*).__
Page 27.

50. **Is the italicized clause dependent or independent?**
I'm tired, *and I'm going home.* _____ dependent ___✔___ independent Page 38.

51. **True or false:**
To turn passive voice verbs active, ask yourself "by whom"; the answer to that question should be the subject. ___✔___ true _____ false
Page 92.

52. **True or false:**
You can justify using plural pronouns with singular subjects to avoid sexist references such as *he.* _____ true ___✓___ false   Page 109.

53. **Is the italicized passage a phrase or a clause?**
It's ironic that Alfred Nobel, *who invented dynamite,* also established the Peace Prize.
_____ phrase ___✓___ clause   Page 38.

54. **Is the italicized word a subject, transitive verb, or direct object?**
Eight *reindeer* pull Santa's sleigh.
___✓___ subject _____ transitive verb _____ direct object   Page 48.

55. **True or false:**
Thoughtful writers *do* repeat key words rather than seeking synonyms.
___✓___ true _____ false   Page 98.

56. **What part of speech is the italicized word?**
The exact delivery date is not certain, *but* we think it will be in two or three weeks.
Conjunction. _____   Page 27.

57. **Is the italicized pronoun used correctly?**
Pollsters are trying to find out *who* New York voters are supporting.
_____ yes ___✓___ no   Page 100.

58. **True or false:**
A clause can always stand alone and make sense. _____ true ___✓___ false
         Page 38.

59. **Should the two parts of the sentence below be separated by a comma?**
Theodore Roosevelt wrote 37 books / but few are well known.
___✓___ yes _____ no   Page 49.

60. **What part of speech is the italicized word?**
What do the letters S.P.C.A. stand *for*? __Preposition.__   Page 27.

61. **Should the two parts of the sentence below be separated by a comma?**
We questioned as many employees as we could / and learned that most union members are for the change. _____ yes ___✓___ no   Page 38.

62. **What part of speech is the italicized clause?**
When the lava came within a mile of the village, the inhabitants were evacuated.
Adverb (modifies *evacuated*). _____   Page 39.

63. **What part of speech are the italicized words?**
The ground ball that drove in the winning run *was ruled* an error.
Verb (passive voice) _____   Page 28.

64. **Should there be a comma at the slash (/) mark?**
Smedley, who won first prize last year / is doing even better so far this year.
___✓___ yes _____ no   Page 78.

Answer Key
to pages 126
through 132

Things you
MUST know

65. **Tell what's wrong with the sentence below, and correct it.**
A minimum of 10 qualifying segments are needed to obtain a free flight certificate.

The error is: ___Subject and verb don't agree.___

Corrected: ___A minimum of 10 qualifying segments is needed . . . .___

___(Singular subject [*minimum*] needs singular verb).___ Page 75.

66. **What part of speech is the italicized word?**
Cappelletti emphasized that the city *wants* the work to continue.
Verb (transitive). Page 28.

67. **Is the italicized clause restrictive or nonrestrictive?**
Crocuses, *although they often bloom before winter ends,* are not affected by cold or snow. _____ restrictive ___✔___ nonrestrictive Page 39.

68. **What part of speech is the italicized clause?**
What goes up must come down. ___Noun (subject).___ Page 39.

69. **True or false:**
Passive voice verbs hinder readers by tempting writers to leave out the words that tell who does what. ___✔___ true _____ false Page 90.

70. **Which is better writing style?**
_____ The branch chief liked the idea. Harry, who was worried about schedules, loved it.

___✔___ The branch chief liked the idea. And Harry, who was worried about schedules, loved it. Page 96.

_____ The branch chief liked the idea, and Harry, who was worried about schedules, loved it.

71. **Is the italicized clause restrictive or nonrestrictive?**
The only machine *that can do this job* is made in Canada.
___✔___ restrictive _____ nonrestrictive Page 39.

72. **True or false:**
The easiest way to avoid sexism in your writing is to switch to the plural.
___✔___ true _____ false Page 108.

73. **What part of speech is the italicized word?**
Political *observers* believe she would be hard put to win any delegates.

Noun (subject). Page 27.

74. **Which is better writing style?**
___✔___ White paint reflects sunlight and also makes most structures seem larger.
Page 52.

_____ White paint, which also makes most structures seem larger, reflects sunlight.

75. **Is the italicized passage a phrase or a clause?**
Ontario is the only Canadian province *that borders the Great Lakes*.
_____ phrase ___✔___ clause   Page 38.

76. **Is the italicized word a subject, transitive verb, or direct object?**
African elephants have larger *ears* than Indian elephants.
_____ subject _____ transitive verb ___✔___ direct object   Page 48.

77. **What part of speech is the italicized word?**
Oh, what a beautiful morning! ___Interjection.___   Page 27.

78. **Tell what's wrong with the sentence below, and correct it.**
After Tommy's successful surgery, Action 4 newscaster Mickey Burrell says, he just wants to go home and get some rest.

The error is called: ___Pronoun with loose antecedent.___

Corrected: ___You can't correct it without more information. As it's written, you___

___can't tell which one wants to go home.___   Page 76.

79. **Is the italicized verb transitive or intransitive?**
Insects *are* the oldest class of animals. _____ transitive ___✔___ intransitive
                                                                   Page 49.

80. **Should the two parts of the sentence below be separated by a comma?**
Oliver Wendell Holmes was a famous Supreme Court Justice / but was never Chief Justice. _____ yes ___✔___ no   Page 49.

81. **Should the two parts of the sentence below be separated by a comma?**
In the seven races of the 1983 Americas Cup Competition / the Australians used an unconventional design and beat the Americans for the first time in a century.
___✔___ yes _____ no   Page 63.

82. **What part of speech is the italicized phrase?**
People *under six feet tall* shouldn't seek careers as basketball players.
___Adjective (modifies *people*).___   Page 37.

83. **What part of speech is the italicized phrase?**
Octopuses, *considered by many to be monsters of the deep,* are actually small and harmless.
___Adjective (modifies *octopuses*).___   Page 37.

84. **Should the two parts of the sentence below be separated by a comma?**
When you left town / things just weren't the same. ___✔___ yes _____ no
                                                                   Page 63.

Answer Key
to pages 126
through 132

Things you
MUST know

85. **Tell what's wrong with the sentence below, and correct it.**
    After spending 20 minutes in the icy water, rescuers finally arrived and pulled the child to safety.

    The error is called: ___Dangling participle._____

    Corrected: ___After the child spent 20 minutes in the icy water, ..._____

    _____(The rescuers weren't in the water; the child was.)_____ Page 74.

86. **Should the two parts of the sentence below be separated by a comma?**
    I would like to thank you for your support / which has been very helpful.
    ___✔___ yes _____ no   Page 63.

87. **What part of speech is the italicized phrase?**
    In accordance with the specifications of your March 16 letter relative to federal regulations governing the import and export of spider eggs, Form 1E 2619-4437-DD-2 is enclosed.
    Adverb (modifies *is enclosed*).   Page 37.

88. **Should there be a comma at the slash (/) mark?**
    The more time zones you cross, and the faster you cross them / the more severe your jet lag is likely to be. ___✔___ yes _____ no   Page 78.

89. **What part of speech is the italicized word?**
    Ask your *department* head for the hospitalization forms.

    Adjective (modifies *head*).   Page 27.

90. **Is the italicized pronoun used correctly?**
    The ideal arrangement would be for Bradley Corp. and *us* to share the work.
    ___✔___ yes _____ no   Page 77.

1. **Should the comma be in the sentence below?**
I ordered fried shrimp, but the waiter brought linguini with clam sauce.
_____✔_____ yes _____ no   Page 63.

2. **What punctuation mark will most effectively separate the parts of the sentence below?**
Research scientists don't like to report details of projects that fail __?__ you can understand why.

Semicolon. _____   Page 64.

3. **Which of these is correctly punctuated?**
_____ Tomorrow we're leaving for London.

_____ Tomorrow, we're leaving for London.

____✔____ Both are correct.   Page 63.

4. **Which of these is correctly punctuated?**
_____ The day after the project is completed and approved by the staff we're leaving
for London.
____✔____ The day after the project is completed and approved by the staff, we're leaving
for London.   Page 63.

5. **Which is correct?**
_____ The Catawba vines were the only ones which survived.

____✔____ The Catawba vines were the only ones that survived.   Page 92.

6. **Which of these is correctly punctuated?**
____✔____ "We were directly involved," the young producer said, "and it was beautiful."
Page 64.

_____ "We were directly involved", the young producer said, "and it was beautiful".

7. **Is the sentence below punctuated correctly?**
The 51 professionals, representing 40 alcoholism and drug treatment agencies were
unanimous that the state isn't doing enough. _____ yes ____✔____ no   Page 78.

8. **Tell what's wrong with the sentence below, and improve it.**
The problems of the Middle East are not without solutions if all involved really want
solutions.

The trouble is. ___Double negative._____

Improved: ___The problems of the Middle East have_____

_____solutions if all . . . .   Page 85.

9. **What punctuation mark is needed between the two parts of the sentence below?**
One point should be obvious to everyone __?__ this machine can't do the job much
longer.

Colon. (Capital T for *This*.) _____   Page 65.

10. **What punctuation mark will best separate the two parts of the sentence below?**
Frogs have teeth __?__ toads do not.   Semicolon._____   Page 65.

Answer Key
to pages 133
through 137

Things you
SHOULD know

11. **Should the comma be in the sentence below?**
    The rain continued all day, and turned to snow just before rush hour.
    _____ yes ___✔___ no   Page 48.

12. **Which of these is correct?**
    _____ None of these has been inspected.
    ___✔___ None of these have been inspected.   Page 75.

13. **True or false:**
    Syntax is the art of building words into effective sentences. ___✔___ true _____ false
    Page 50.

14. **Which of these is correct?**
    ___✔___ Several of your findings are different from ours.   Page 78.
    _____ Several of your findings are different than ours.

15. **Which of these is correctly punctuated?**
    _____ Wallpaper, carpeting and drapes have not been installed yet.
    ___✔___ Wallpaper, carpeting, and drapes have not been installed yet.   Page 63.

16. **Tell what's wrong with the sentence below, and correct it.**
    Bianca can play flute, piano, guitar, and sing second soprano.

    The error is called: ____False series._____

    Corrected: ____Bianca can play flute, piano, and guitar. She_____

    _____can also sing . . . ._____ Page 77.

17. **Which of these is correctly punctuated?**
    _____ One of the contestants is my brother; therefore I shouldn't be a judge.
    ___✔___ One of the contestants is my brother; therefore, I shouldn't be a judge.
    Page 97.

18. **What is the structure of the sentence below?**
    Anyone who can't swim should learn how.
    _____ simple _____ compound ___✔___ complex   Page 49.

19. **Which of these is correct?**
    ___✔___ The 16-bit system, which uses interactive software programs, allows us to add terminals later.   Page 92.
    _____ The 16-bit system, that uses interactive software programs, allows us to add terminals later.

20. **What punctuation marks will most effectively separate the parts of the sentence below?**
    If you want to improve your computer skills ___?___ and I know you do ___?___ you should attend this seminar.

    ____Dashes._____   Page 65.

21. **What punctuation mark is needed between the two parts of the sentence below?**
Franklin D. Roosevelt was president of the U.S. longer than any other person __?__ he served 3-1/2 terms, for 13 years.

Semicolon. _____   Page 64.

22. **What is the structure of the sentence below?**
I'm tired, and I'm hungry.
___✔___ compound   _____ complex   _____ compound/complex   Page 49.

23. **What punctuation mark will best separate the two parts of the sentence below?**
Chief Justice Warren Burger is critical of American lawyers __?__ he thinks they lack civility.

Semicolon. _____   Page 64.

24. **Tell what's wrong with the sentence below, and improve it.**
It would not have been surprising if Yarborough had not done well that day.

The trouble is: ___Double negative._____

Improved: ___It would not have been surprising if Yarborough_____

_____had done badly that day._____   Page 85.

25. **What punctuation mark is needed between the two parts of the sentence below?**
Only one National Football League team does not have decorations on the sides of its helmets __?__ the Cleveland Browns.

Colon. _____   Page 65.

26. **Which of these is correct?**
_____ The central processing unit has 2 disk drives.
___✔___ The central processing unit has two disk drives.   Page 114.

27. **Should the comma be in the sentence below?**
The hospital is overcrowded, and patient care has suffered as a result.
___✔___ yes   _____ no   Page 63.

28. **Which of these is correct?**
___✔___ The system now has 27 terminals.   Page 114.
_____ The system now has twenty-seven terminals.

29. **Tell what's wrong with the sentence below, and correct it.**
We can only assure you that these changes were observed regularly in the findings.

The trouble is: ___Wandering *only*._____

Corrected: ___We can assure you only that these findings . . . .____   Page 52.

30. **True or false:**
Use *that* for restrictive clauses and *which* for nonrestrictive. ___✓___ true _____ false
Page 92.

31. **What punctuation mark is needed between the two parts of the sentence below?**
Albert Blake Dick invented the mimeograph machine __?__ and the A. B. Dick Co. is named after him.

Comma. _____ Page 49.

32. **What is the structure of the sentence above?**
_____ simple ___✓___ compound _____ complex Page 49.

33. **Tell what's wrong with the sentence below, and correct it.**

Certificates will only be issued to registered contestants.

The trouble is: ___Wandering *only*.___

Corrected: ___Certificates will be issued only to . . . .___ Page 52.

34. **Correct the sentence below.**
Hopefully, you'll be able to join me this week-end.
I hope you'll be able to join me . . . . Page 49.

35. **True or false:**
A prepositional phrase always serves as an adjective or an adverb.
___✓___ true _____ false Page 37.

36. **What punctuation would be most effective between the two parts of the sentence below?**
California does not have the longest coastline of any U.S. state __?__ Alaska has.

Semicolon. _____ Page 64.

37. **Tell what's wrong with the sentence below, and correct it.**
A well-dressed woman only wears diamonds at night.

The error is called: ___Wandering *only*.___

Corrected: ___A well-dressed woman wears diamonds___

___only at night.___ Page 52.

38. **What punctuation mark would be most effective between the two parts of the sentence below?**
Upward-curved corners on Chinese roofs serve an important purpose __?__ they keep evil spirits away.

Colon. (Capital T for *They*) _____ Page 65.

39. **Tell what's wrong with the sentence below, and correct it.**
Once we were able to actually administer the venum, the child's condition began to quickly stabilize.

The errors are called: ___Split infinitive (two)._____

Corrected: ___Once we were actually able to administer the venum, the_____

___child's condition began to stabilize quickly._____ Page 40.

40. **True or false:**
Passive voice verbs are a bit dull because the subject receives the action rather than performing it. __✔__ true _____ false   Page 90.

41. **True or false:**
A clause doesn't need a subject or a verb, but a phrase needs both.
_____ true __✔__ false   Pages 37, 38.

42. **Should the comma be in the sentence below?**
The maintenance representative still hasn't arrived, but has promised to be here first thing tomorrow morning. _____ yes __✔__ no   Page 48.

43. **Which of these is correct?**
_____ Uniplan is hard disk system.
__✔__ Uniplan is a hard-disk system.   Page 66.

44. **True or false:**
Who's Who should be *Who's Whom.* _____ true __✔__ false   Page 77.

Answer Key
to pages 133
through 137

*Things you
SHOULD know*

1. **English is in the family of languages called:**
   _____ Romance   __✓__ Teutonic   _____ Anglo-Saxon   Page 15.

2. **The person who most affected the development of English is:**
   _____ Shakespeare   _____ King James   __✓__ William the Conqueror
                                                              Page 16.

3. **English grammar is in the category called:**
   __✓__ Syntactical   _____ Inflectional   _____ Transitive   Page 18.

4. **That means:**
   _____ Nouns and pronouns don't have gender (sex).
   _____ Every sentence must have a subject and verb.
   __✓__ The role of words is determined by their positions.   Page 18.

5. **True or false: English is known for the ease with which it accepts change.**
   __✓__ true   _____ false   Page 18.

6. **The most famous literary work from the Old English period is:**
   _____ The vulgate Bible   __✓__ Beowulf   _____ The Canterbury Tales
                                                              Page 15.

7. **Old English was a mixture of:**
   __✓__ Gaelic and Teutonic   Page 15.
   _____ Anglo-Saxon and Latin
   _____ Anglo-Saxon and French

8. **English grammar is known for its:**
   __✓__ Simplicity   _____ Complexity   _____ Poetic choices   Page 19.

9. **True or false:**
   English uses the Roman alphabet because it is best suited for a language of such diverse characteristics.
   _____ true   __✓__ false   Page 14.

10. **Middle English was a mixture of:**
    _____ Gaelic and Latin
    __✓__ Anglo-Saxon and French   Page 17.
    _____ Anglo-Saxon and Latin

11. **The works of Shakespeare are hard to understand today because:**
    _____ We are unaccustomed to the word order of sentences ending with verbs.
    _____ He wrote for the wealthy aristocrats of the London court.
    __✓__ English has changed so much since the Elizabethan Age.   Page 16.

12. **True or false:**
    What Americans think of as a British accent is a relatively new style of pronunciation. The pilgrims on the Mayflower spoke an English that sounded much like today's American English.
    __✓__ true   _____ false   Page 19.

Index

Index

The Writing Course That Made History

Participants' Manuals One for each person taking the course. A complete working guide and permanent reference, containing text and practice materials.

Course Outline:
PART ONE

SESSION 1:
"Clarity – Your First Objective." Introduction, and the first two of Mr. Joseph's Six Principles of Clear Writing.

SESSION 2:
"Changing Some Old Attitudes." The remaining four principles of clarity. Exploding some widespread language myths and replacing them with modern, sensible viewpoints.

SESSION 3:
"Measuring Your Clarity." The Robert Gunning Fog Index. How important is brevity? Habits of legal and scientific writers.

Put It In Writing
by Albert Joseph

Now Also
- **One-Day Workshop**
- **Engineering Edition**

BENEFITS

CLARITY – Your employees will learn how to write so clearly *and accurately* their readers cannot possibly misunderstand.

ORGANIZATION – They will learn how to organize (and outline) for the reader's needs, following simple yet sensible guidelines.

COURTESY – They will learn how to present their valuable ideas in a language style that pleases the reader and creates a pleasant, dignified image of your organization.

SPEED – Knowing how to do these things will help them write quickly, confidently, without fumbling over false starts and rewrites.

These benefits apply to all kinds of writing: reports, letters, procedures, or memos – technical or nontechnical.

Leader's Guide So thorough *anyone* can teach writing: no background is needed as either a writer or a trainer.

Course Outline:
PART TWO

SESSION 4:
"Practical Tips on Organizing." The inverted pyramid structure (conclusion first). A checklist to evaluate structure.

SESSION 5:
"How to Outsmart the Deadline." Surprisingly effective (and well received) advice on one of the key points in writing: the outline. Guidelines for nonsexist writing.

SESSION 6:
"The Finishing Touches of the Pros." Use of headings. The importance of white space. Advice on letters. Dictation. Reviewing and editing the writing of others. What computers can (and can't) do for your writing.

Available:
• Self-Study Programs
• Government Edition

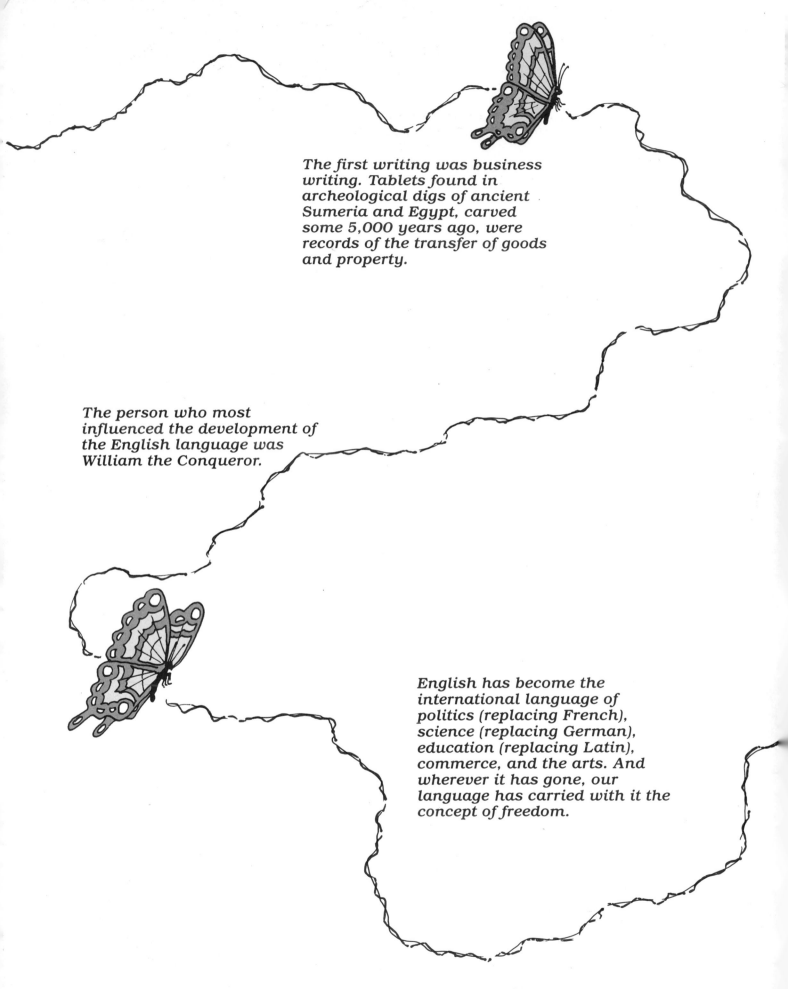

The first writing was business writing. Tablets found in archeological digs of ancient Sumeria and Egypt, carved some 5,000 years ago, were records of the transfer of goods and property.

The person who most influenced the development of the English language was William the Conqueror.

English has become the international language of politics (replacing French), science (replacing German), education (replacing Latin), commerce, and the arts. And wherever it has gone, our language has carried with it the concept of freedom.

Book Design & Illustration: Paula L. Grooms / Design Works